KEN AND ME

Ken
and Me

WILLIAM ROACHE

with
Stan Nicholls

SIMON & SCHUSTER

LONDON·SYDNEY·NEW YORK·TOKYO·SINGAPORE·TORONTO

First published in Great Britain by Simon & Schuster Ltd, 1993
A Paramount Communications Company

Copyright ©William Roache, 1993

Simon & Schuster Ltd
West Garden Place
Kendal Street
London W2 2AQ

Simon & Schuster of Australia Pty Ltd
Sydney

A CIP catalogue record for this book is available from the British Library.

ISBN 0–671–71213–6

Typeset in Sabon
by Hewer Text Composition Services, Edinburgh
Printed in Great Britain by
Butler & Tanner Ltd, Frome and London

To Sara, Verity, William
and all the animals for the love and
distractions of family life

Acknowledgements

This book is all from memory with no research other than a few dates from the Ministry of Defence so there may well be some inaccuracies for which I apologise: my memory was never my strong point.

I would like to thank life for the experiences it has provided for me and my parents for preparing me to meet them.

Granada for being through most of my adult life not only my employer but also my guide and protector in so many ways.

Simon & Schuster for jolting me sufficiently out of my lethargy to start writing this book.

Stan Nicholls for being so sympathetic and understanding under pressure to give this book its shape.

One

'Why do you always have to be so different, Roache?'

The question took me by surprise. Unable to reply, I simply stared at Dr Britten until he turned and walked away.

It was never my intention to be different. In fact I was rather shy and easily given to blushing. But I knew what the duty master meant.

It wasn't just that he had found me bouncing a tennis ball against an outbuilding while everyone else at Rydal School was attending Sunday morning service. Nor the fact that although I played the trumpet and was in the dramatic society I also turned out for Rydal's cricket and rugby teams. It wasn't that I was totally and unrepentantly left-handed. Or even that I was a persistent bed-wetter until the age of ten.

It was as if he had looked into the depths of my being and seen something there.

I was aware of that *something* too. Call it a sense of destiny, a vocation or a mission; call it what you will, I knew I would recognise my purpose in life when I saw it, and devote myself wholeheartedly to its fulfilment.

I still have that feeling.

I was born on the 23rd of April, 1932. Or was it the 25th? I honestly don't know. It must be quite an achievement to have a copy of your birth certificate and still not know the day you were born.

Up to the age of eighteen my birthday was celebrated on the 23rd of April. That year, 1950, my school rugby team was drawn to play Belvedere College in Ireland, and each member of the First Fifteen had to apply for a passport.

'I don't believe it!' my father exclaimed when he finally located my birth certificate in the dining room cupboard. 'Your birthday isn't on the 23rd, it's on the 25th.'

The certificate is dated the 25th, but I think the registrar made a mistake in also writing that as the date of my birth. The actual date of birth would have been a couple of days earlier. Years later, when an interest in astrology required establishing the exact time and place of my birth, I tried a little detective work. The maternity home where I was born and their records no longer existed, and trying to stir my parents' memories of events thirty-five years before, even on as important a topic as the day of my arrival, proved equally fruitless. So I believe my real birthday to be the 23rd of April. But my 'official' birthday, so to speak, is the 25th.

And all I can remember about playing rugby against Belvedere College was being horribly sick on the night crossing from Holyhead.

My childhood was spent at Rutland House, the family home in Ilkeston, Derbyshire, and in the garden there I first had the conviction I was going to do something meaningful. This was so strong, that I resolved to become a missionary doctor in China. In the event, I was destined to follow a different path but, as I said, that feeling of my life not having really started yet, and the sense of an uncompleted purpose, still persists.

That garden seemed huge when I was a child. In its centre was a large weeping ash under which my sister Beryl and I had a sand pit and swing; in the summer it was like being in a wonderful leafy world all of our own.

At the end of the drive leading to the garden were some

rather grand iron gates. On the right-hand brick gatepost were two brass plates. The top one read DOCTOR W.H. ROACHE, who was my grandfather. The other read DOCTOR W.V. ROACHE – my father. I think it was always assumed there would be a third reading DOCTOR W.P. ROACHE. But all I inherited from my ancestors was hypochondria and bad handwriting.

The house itself was early Victorian, built on to an old cottage, with a lean-to conservatory on the other side in which a grapevine grew. This was part of the waiting room for my father's surgery, and it was quite usual, and permissible, for patients to help themselves to the grapes.

In the old cottage part of the house there was an ancient, unused well, covered by a square flagstone with an iron handle. The family joke was that this was where the doctors hid their mistakes! However, it was in the bathroom directly above this, when I was about fourteen, that I think I saw my one and only ghost.

It was broad daylight. I was sitting on the loo, facing the open door, when a figure appeared in front of me. It had what I can only describe as the classic spook shape – a dark grey, sheet-like outline with yellow eyes. This apparition stood between me and the only way out of the bathroom, and, needless to say, I was petrified. But after a few seconds it vanished. I never saw it again or mentioned the incident to anyone.

A long, unlit corridor connected this bathroom to the main house, and Beryl and I had to cross it on our way to bed. She used to say, 'I dare you to go and switch the bathroom light on.' Not wishing to be thought cowardly, I would take a deep breath, dash down the corridor to the light switch and tear back again. I always fell for it. Because, of course, Beryl was just as frightened as I was.

Apart from our parents and Beryl, who is three years older than me, the household included a maid and another doctor acting as my father's assistant. And at any given time there would usually be an elderly relative seeing out their days.

My maternal grandmother Zilla was a good business woman. After many years of running a shop in Blackpool she took over Alton Towers, when it ceased to be the family home of the Earl of Shrewsbury, and ran it as a bar and restaurant. I remember playing there as a small child. Seeing it today as one of the biggest theme parks it amuses me to think that it was my grandmother who started it off as a place of entertainment. She lived at Rutland House until her death in hospital from cancer. My maternal grandfather Albert, who drank a lot, I heard had occasionally beaten Zilla and been very cool towards my mother. Beryl once chased me down the garden with a piece of cold tripe that Albert always had for his supper. She threw it at me, missed, and after we had washed out the gravel we innocently watched him eat it. While we were away at school he committed suicide at Rutland House by cutting his throat with a razor; he took two days to die. My father nursed him but my mother never saw him during those two days.

Then there was Uncle John.

Uncle John was my father's younger brother. Having had rheumatic fever as a boy, my father was not allowed to engage in strenuous activities or sports, and he channelled his energies into qualifying as a doctor. Uncle John, on the other hand, was the dashing extrovert; handsome, good at cricket, football and swimming, bright at his schoolwork and popular with the girls.

In my father's last year at St Bartholomew's, shortly before he was due to take his finals, my grandfather died. Three days later my grandmother followed him. Both had succumbed to influenza. My father had to rush home to sort things out before sitting his finals. He then got married, had a quick honeymoon in Matlock and immediately took over grandfather's practice.

Uncle John, meanwhile, had just started his first year at Bart's, and was living on an allowance provided by my father. During the holidays John would visit Rutland House and report on his progress. This went on for about four years. Then one day he announced he had failed his finals for the second time and needed to stay on for another year. Father contacted St Bartholomew's and was staggered to discover Uncle John had in reality been kicked out three years earlier.

My father had been deceived. John had blown his allowance living the high life in London. Worse, he had become an alcoholic.

The family rallied round. Uncle John's engagement to a beautiful young woman called Molly was broken off, and it was decided he should go into the Army. The local vicar, the Reverend Butterton, put his immortal soul at risk by writing John a glowing testimonial which helped get him into the Royal Medical Corps. He worked his way through the ranks and became a quartermaster. This was against all the odds, and it was generally assumed it must have been the war that got him promotion rather than the dismissal we all expected.

He continued to visit during his periods of leave, and I was always finding empty bottles around the house when he was there. I can see him now, swaying in a doorway, red-eyed, as my mother lectured him. When he came home, things like soap and toothpaste would go missing, but the last straw was when my father watched him take some money from a wallet in his jacket pocket. From then on his visits were restricted.

His forty-fifth birthday, in 1950, marked his dreaded retirement from the Army. Although he could ill-afford it, my father paid him half the value of Rutland House, and the hope was that John would find himself employment and a place to live.

He surprised us by joining Alcoholics Anonymous and drying out. He got a job, a horrid little room in Nottingham, and formed a relationship with a prostitute who apparently charged him for her services. So whereas before he borrowed and stole money for drink, he now did it for sex.

He suffered from emphysema for some time, but continued smoking, eventually dying of lung cancer in 1975 at the age of seventy.

Uncle John caused a lot of unhappiness for my parents. My mother told me he tried to make love to her on one occasion, and that he had seduced a fourteen-year-old cousin who was staying in the house. I later discovered that on his deathbed my grandfather had made my father promise to look after John. This, and my father's innate kindness, explained why he found it so difficult to refuse his younger brother anything.

Despite his roguish behaviour, and all the problems he created, my lasting memory of Uncle John is somewhat affectionate. He was certainly lively company.

Those elderly relatives I mentioned who shared Rutland House with us from time to time included my Great Aunt Ede. Auntie Ede was small, thin, probably in her seventies and a really nice old dear. She was in the room next to mine, where she spent all day reading, smoking and drinking a medicinal burgundy, for which she would dispatch me to the chemist with great frequency.

It was during the war, when I was eleven or twelve and home from school during the summer holidays, that one morning my mother woke me with a cup of tea. This was unprecedented. She put the cup down, said, 'I'm afraid Aunt Ede is dead,' and left the room. The cup of tea was intended for Ede.

I got up and slowly dressed, thinking of Auntie Ede lying next door. Everyone else was downstairs, but before joining them, I hesitated. Should I go in and say goodbye to her? I had never seen anyone dead before and didn't know how I would feel about it.

After deliberating for quite a while I resolved to see her. I opened the door, went in, and was relieved to find Auntie Ede looking as if she was peacefully asleep. 'Bye bye, Auntie,' I whispered softly. Then I thought, I wonder if she used up her sweet coupons? Such are the priorities of youth.

A large drawer under her wardrobe was later found to be full of empty burgundy bottles, and the room smelled of tobacco for years afterwards.

Sadly, due to their comparatively early deaths, I never met my paternal grandparents. My grandmother was also an alcoholic, which may have contributed to her son John's predilection for drink, and there were scratches inside the cellar door at Rutland House said to have been made by her fingernails. But alcoholism apart, she was apparently a delightful and vivacious person.

My grandfather was a much-loved doctor in the old tradition, who would often be called out just to settle family arguments. He was, alas, a hopeless businessman, and my father inherited large debts along with the practice. Not only would my grandfather neglect to send bills for his services, but during the Great Depression families visited by him would like as not find five shillings on their table after he had left. He was talked about with great respect and affection.

But his generosity of spirit was not the only reason I was sad not to have met him. When I began to have an interest in alternative medicines and mysticism, my father more than once remarked that I sounded just like my grandfather. He was interested in homoeopathy, hypnotism, spiritualism and theosophy. He was also a Freemason. I was told he spent many an evening with the Reverend Butterton, drinking claret and discussing things metaphysical into the small hours.

My father was quite different in nature, sharing none of these interests, but was an equally kind and much-loved man. Unfortunately there was never the closeness between us I would have liked, partly due to the incredible demands made by pre National Health Service general practice, and partly because I went away to boarding school at a very early age.

As well as being on call twenty-four hours a day, he also did his own dispensing. In the cellar were shelves and cupboards holding bottles filled with pills and liquids from which he would make up the prescriptions for his patients. These would be laid on a table in the hall waiting for collection, alongside a slate on which were written the names and addresses of the house calls he had to make.

The doorbell and telephone rang all day long, and often my sister and I would take turns answering them. But this task was made harder the moment Beryl discovered my weakness. I was an inveterate giggler. And contrary to my public image, still am. In fact, there was a time when I thought professional acting was out of the question because of it.

Almost anything would set me off. All Beryl had to do was make a nasal sniggering noise and I was away. When it was my turn to answer the door she would stand behind a curtain in the hall and make this noise. I would find myself politely listening to the caller talking about some dreadful illness and trying desperately not to dissolve. Usually I failed, much to the embarrassment of the patient and myself.

One evening we were particularly bad and father had given us a warning about it. I pleaded with Beryl to give me a break but, as all gigglers know, the more serious the situation the bigger the giggle. Then the doorbell rang. With a final plea for mercy, I walked down the hall and opened the door.

'Good evening,' I said.

'Good evening,' the man on the doorstep replied. 'Could I see the doctor please?'

'Certainly. Who shall I say is calling?'

'Mr Onions.'

That did it. I was gone. Leaving the man standing at the

door I staggered to the drawing room and collapsed into convulsive laughter.

After a while I composed myself somewhat and asked Beryl if she would tell father there was someone to see him. She refused. So I did my best to look sombre, knocked on the surgery door and went in.

'Yes?' said my father, as he and his patient turned to look at me.

'There's a Mr . . . er . . . um . . . a Mr . . . and I burst into a new round of uncontrollable mirth. Unable to speak, I fled father's office. He stormed out after me, absolutely furious, and gave the pair of us the biggest ticking-off of our lives.

Sadly, even that didn't cure me, and giggling has proved a bane of my life to this day.

My hypochondria manifested itself early, too. On one occasion I convinced myself I had some terrible problem with my heart. I just knew it was going to stop at any minute and for days was resigned to the fact that this was the end. I crept around gingerly, sure that any sudden movement would bring on a seizure. Eventually I decided to break the news of my imminent demise to father.

'I'm afraid there's something awfully wrong with my heart,' I announced.

My father looked at me for a moment then said, 'Come here.'

Tentatively, I moved towards him. Without warning he shoved me hard in the chest, sending me crashing back against the wall. My God! I thought, he's killed me! But, realising I was still alive, my terror was quickly replaced by anger.

I didn't have time to voice my mounting resentment, because father added, 'There's nothing wrong with you, and I've got enough problems without the family adding to them.'

I strode out of the surgery thinking, that's great! A doctor who doesn't care about his family. It was quite a while before I calmed down enough to realise I was feeling fine. My father was a good psychologist.

He employed a diverse assortment of assistants over the years, and the longest-serving was Dr Gunter, an energetic man with a decidedly bizarre sense of humour. One of my abiding memories of him was that he took up a new sport or hobby on practically a weekly basis, but rarely got beyond reading a book on the subject.

One evening, while we were sitting around the dining room table eating supper, Dr Gunter came in wearing his white coat and carrying a small bottle. This apparently contained someone's urine sample. He removed the cork, held up the bottle so we could all see it and said, 'A little cloudy, don't you think?' Then he downed the content in a gulp. There was a stunned silence as he left the room.

To our relief, we later discovered the bottle had held some homemade wine given to him by one of the patients.

There is a tragic footnote to Dr Gunter's story, however. A few years after this event he was committed to a mental institution where he stayed for the rest of his life. This was nothing to do with the urine incident, I hasten to add, which I relate as an example of his excellent, if rather black, sense of humour.

Another eccentric character ever-present during my childhood years at Rutland House was Mr Beardsley, the gardener. He was an old, red-haired man who always wore a bowler hat, and he kept the garden beautifully.

One day, when I was playing on the lawn, he called me over. He took five small sticks and arranged them in a row at our feet, thus:

$$| \quad | \quad | \quad | \quad |$$

'Move two of those sticks and make the best drink in the world,' he said. I stared at them blankly for a few minutes.

Then he moved the two outside sticks and placed them horizontally over the ones next to them, making:

and immediately went into a long wheezing laugh.

I walked away really puzzled by this. How could a bird possibly be a drink?

Two

I was four-and-a-half years old when the words that change every child's life were addressed to me.

'Come on,' mother said, 'You're going to school.'

Hand in hand, we set off down the drive, and after about ten minutes reached a terraced house in nearby Lord Haddon Road. The door was opened by a woman of whom I have no recollection whatsoever, and we were ushered into the front room, or what in those days was often called the parlour. This had been converted into a classroom. It was, in fact, the whole school.

There were two wooden desks with attached bench-seats, one behind the other, each able to accommodate six children. The entire complement of pupils, seven or eight in all, was crawling on the floor under these desks. None of my prospective schoolmates reacted to our entrance, but after some rather feeble entreaties from the unmemorable lady, things settled down a little. She started to talk, but I was only aware of occasional phrases. 'Welcome to Chilwel House . . . the doctor's son . . . joining us . . . will be happy . . .'

Apart from fragments of that introduction I remember nothing at all about my short time at that particular school. But then my education took a much more interesting turn.

My grandfather's interest in theosophy, the movement founded by Rudolf Steiner, led him and a fellow enthusiast called Miss Lewis to establish a Steiner school next door to Rutland House. Indeed he gave over a large part of the garden to this venture. So it was perhaps inevitable, even though neither of my parents had any understanding of Steiner's philosophy, that I should become a pupil at Michael House. It was a wise decision. My two-and-a-half years there proved the happiest of all my school days.

Getting to school was a doddle. Out of the gate, turn left and left again. If late, over the wall. This became so casual and automatic that one day, sitting in the classroom, I realised I was still wearing my bedroom slippers.

Rudolf Steiner schools worked towards developing harmonised individuals, with music and art regarded as of greater value than academic facts. There were no punishments that I remember, but responsibility for your own actions and caring for others were impressed from the beginning. Nor was there any overt religious teaching. But a strong spiritual air permeated everything we did. The place was full of music, light, colour, and kindness.

One teacher took you right through the school, and mine was Mrs Price. Her auburn hair was gathered at the back in a bun, but this was not austere, and she had a round, kindly face more often than not lit by a smile.

Eurhythmic dancing was an important part of the curriculum, and this was taken by Miss Green, whose long, dark hair framed a pale, oval face with almond eyes, high cheekbones and a full mouth. She wore floor-length dresses and sandals, making her look like a hippie before her time.

It was at Michael House that I first appeared on stage. The school put on regular theatrical displays, which could be called the Steiner equivalent of nativity plays, and I featured in one as a tree – an oak, if memory serves me. This necessitated standing in the background with my arms outstretched for what seemed like an eternity. I began to understand why standing with your arms outstretched for long periods is a recognised form of torture. But I found it was possible to give myself some support by pinching the drapes behind me with two fingers of each hand.

Unfortunately, this caused the drapes to fall down and brought the show to an abrupt end.

My mother, who was in the audience, was cross with me for this. Not just because of bringing the drapes down, but because it had spoilt my performance. So I learned a valuable lesson from that first public appearance: it doesn't matter if you ruin the whole production as long as your own performance is good.

It was after two years at Michael House, when I was approaching the age of seven, that the gathering clouds of war finally burst.

I clearly remember sitting with the family in the drawing room listening to Neville Chamberlain's announcement on the wireless that we were at war with Germany. After the broadcast, my parents talked very quietly and seriously for some time, mainly about the possibility of my father being called up to serve in the Army. In the event he was not called, but stayed to run Ilkeston Hospital, and to work with the local Air Raid Precaution group.

We were all issued with gasmasks. My father's filled me with envy. It had two round, goggle-like eyepieces and a ribbed rubber tube leading down to a filter canister held in a canvas case. By contrast, Beryl and I had the simple blunt-nosed type with a rectangle of clear celluloid to see through, and they had to be carried in a cardboard box suspended from our necks by a piece of string.

There were blackout precautions, of course, and all the windows had to be covered with heavy curtains or blinds. In addition to this, every house had to provide a safe place to act as an air raid shelter. My parents decided the kitchen would be our safe place and strong steel shutters were fixed to this room's only window. On many occasions after the air raid siren sounded we would sit around the kitchen fire drinking Ovaltine and listening to the radio. It was cosy, and fun, especially if it was in the middle of the night.

Our kitchen was no safer than any other room. If a bomb had landed on or near the house we would have been buried in a pile of rubble. But someone had decided we were going to have a comfortable war, rather than a safe war.

We soon fell into a routine, and part of this was the Monday morning ritual of walking up Bath Street at the far end of town to visit Keightly's grocery shop. The beige ration books were handed over and marked, or pieces cut out with a large pair of scissors. Then the detailed weighing of each item and the scooping of sugar into thick, blue paper bags began.

When this was completed Mr Keightly would direct 'the look' at us. There followed a discrete wink, and the production from under the counter of some well-wrapped, specially saved titbit no ration book could buy. This was the real reason we made the long trek past many another grocer to Keightly's at the top of town.

Everyone was expected to do their bit, and I remember the sadness I felt as I watched Rutland House's magnificent gates being taken away, never to be replaced, as part of the war effort.

The Roache family's war effort also included giving over the garden to flocks of ducks and hens. They wandered freely, scratching up the flower beds, and frequently walked down the now gateless drive and on to the road. As they had no special nesting boxes, one of my jobs was to hunt down new nests and collect the eggs.

These birds had voracious appetites, as I discovered one summer evening while I sat listening to an Al Jolson record on the wind-up gramophone. The stylus needed changing and, finding a little tin full of old needles, I unthinkingly threw them out of the drawing room window. They were immediately gobbled up by a pack of greedy hens. They may have looked like golden corn but I doubt they tasted as good. I watched the hens and their eggs with interest and more than a little anxiety over the next few days, but there were no apparent ill-effects.

On another occasion my mother brought in a dozen day-old chicks which had been kept inside in the airing cupboard. It was a warm sunny day and she decided to give them their first run in the garden while she went shopping. I was left in charge with strict orders not to let them out of my sight.

The twelve bright yellow chicks trotted around in a group for a while. Suddenly, one of them broke ranks. It staggered to the left; it staggered to the right. Then it fell on its back with its feet in the air. I picked it up and ran into the kitchen with it. I put water on its beak in an attempt to revive it, but it was a lost cause. Laying it on the draining-board, I went back outside to keep my eye on the others.

I arrived just in time to see a repeat performance. One of them broke away, staggered to the left, then to the right and finally collasped with its feet in the air. I took this one inside too and tried the same life-saving procedure. But to no avail. I left it on the draining-board next to the first chick.

A third pegged out in exactly the same way the minute I stepped back into the garden. Their timing was impeccable. Each time I emerged from the house another one gave up the ghost. Eventually there were eleven lifeless chicks on the draining-board, and I was following the last one around the garden with mounting apprehension, hoping that at least *it* would be alive when mother got back from shopping. Alas, this was not to be, and I had to break the sad news on her return.

My mother, never one to cry over spilt milk, immediately joined a pig club.

One or two bombs were dropped on Ilkeston, but they were thought to be from planes offloading to get home more quickly after raiding the Rolls Royce factories in Derby, some ten miles away.

What happened next could have resulted from my parents' fear of these bombings. It could have been because I had chest trouble, sometimes waking up in the morning hardly able to breathe. It could have been that they were prepared to make a big sacrifice in order to give me the best start in life, or even that they would do anything for a bit of peace and quiet. Whatever the reason, they decided to send me away to boarding school at the tender age of seven.

My cousin Harry was at Rydal School in Colwyn Bay, North Wales; his sister Audrey was at Penrhos in the same town. This connection, and the fact that Colwyn Bay was a healthy place and safe from the war, were the reasons why Rydal was chosen for me and Penrhos for Beryl.

The long, tedious car journey from Ilkeston to Colwyn Bay was completed, and we dropped off Beryl at Penrhos first. After a tearful goodbye to her it was my turn and we set out for Rydal School. Or so I thought. I was a little surprised, though not at all displeased, when my father turned the car into the driveway of a nearby hotel. Beryl's term started a day before mine and my parents didn't want her to know in case she got upset. So we had a pleasant night in the hotel and I got a day's reprieve.

Morning, and the short drive to Beech House, home of Rydal Junior School, arrived all too soon.

We were greeted by a lady of indeterminate age in a dark-blue uniform, white starched cap and apron. 'Good morning,' she said, 'I'm Matron. Do come in.' She led us through the porch into a large wood-panelled room with an ornate fireplace and parquet flooring. A wide staircase swept down from an open landing.

Matron was upright without being rigid, and although not cosy or cuddly I did not feel threatened by her. In fact I quite liked her. As we walked up the stairs together, she said, 'I'll show you your dormitory and then you must say goodbye to your mother and father.' We entered a light room with a bay window and the smell of polish in the air. There were six unsprung iron beds with a small locker by each, and every bed was covered by a woollen travelling rug supplied by the boys. My bed was instantly recognisable by the dark-blue tartan rug that was to stay with me to the end of my school days.

The time came to kiss my parents goodbye, and I watched from the window as they got into their car and drove away. I didn't cry, but I did feel sad and a little frightened.

As the day wore on, and more and more boys arrived, the decibel level gradually rose. Boys always seem to make more noise on the first day of term than at any other time; in truth they probably *do* make more noise due to excitement and fear.

That first night was strange, and the unfamiliar bed was hard and uncomfortable. But with Matron looking after the new intake of first year boys, it was only a few days before I adjusted.

However, something strange, almost prophetic, occurred on that first day. The system was that new arrivals were handed over to a senior boy who would show them the ropes and generally look after them. Mine was called John Howarth. He arrived with his father, this little, round, potato-shaped chap called Jack Howarth, who ran the theatre repertory company in Colwyn Bay. I remember being very impressed by the ivory-topped cane he carried.

'What's your name?' he said.

'Billy Roache.'

'And where do you come from?'

After a suitable pause for thought I replied, 'England.'

He thought that was very funny. We laughed about it again twenty years later, when Jack played Ken's uncle Albert in *Coronation Street*.

The older boys took meals in the dining hall on long refectory tables; we had a smaller table in a separate room with Matron at its head. Rice pudding, semolina and sago were invariably served, and Matron would walk around the table very slowly, keeping a strict eye on us to see that we ate it all.

I recall a meal, shortly after my arrival, when Matron spent some time hovering over the boy sitting opposite me while he forced down one or two spoonfuls of semolina. As she moved to the far end of the table he spewed it back into his bowl. On Matron's second circuit she stopped beside him and said, 'We don't seem to be making much progress, do we, McGowan?'

He looked up at her with fear-filled eyes.

'There are children all over the world who are starving,' she continued. 'Now come along, eat up.'

Tears were rolling down poor McGowan's cheeks by this time and he was unable to speak.

'Look, I'll help you,' Matron said brightly, dipping his spoon into the secondhand semolina and holding it to his trembling lips.

The rest of us sat in fascinated silence, far from ideal companions in McGowan's time of need, as the spoon was placed against his mouth and tilted.

'That's not too bad now, is it?' said Matron.

He was sick all over the table.

I thank my lucky stars semolina is so unfashionable these days. If it weren't, and somebody served it to me at a dinner party, I think it would present a bit of a problem.

Matron also supervised each evening's bathing sessions. She sat perched on a chair with a large pile of towels by her and three of us sat one behind the other in the white enamel bath. After a few minutes of washing with a piece of what passed for soap, we stood up, had a towel placed over our shoulders and walked out as the next three came in.

In the summer we had to take a cold bath in the mornings. A line of naked boys formed in the corridor outside the bathroom and went in one at a time. We had to totally submerge ourselves, and if this was not achieved to Matron's satisfaction it had to be done again.

It was hell.

Far from building my character and making me a hardy member of the British Empire ready to fight for King and Country, it turned me into a hothouse plant who won't swim unless the pool is steaming, and whose central heating is kept on all year round.

For some reason I was unable to discover, we all called Matron 'Tronna'. Although never to her face, of course. Where this name came from I have no idea. Possibly it was derived in some curious way from 'Matron'. Or it may have been a corruption of her real name, which I never knew.

On the subject of nicknames, I had one myself for a time at Rydal, thanks to Mr Lewis, the junior school headmaster. We were sitting at table with him after supper one evening when he remarked, 'Did you know that a roach is a fish?' Everybody looked at me. 'I think Roache should be called fish, don't you?' So it was for all my junior schooldays. Fortunately it was dropped when I reached the senior school.

No doubt, on encountering an Old Boy from the junior school, he would find some difficulty in suppressing the urge to call me Fishy Roache. Indeed, I remember being on some railway station platform once, seeing a respectable middle-aged man surrounded by his loving family, and blurting out, 'Hello, Banana!'

Meeting the chemistry master from the senior school, 'Shitto' Osborne, would have been an even greater hazard.

The first form was taken for all its lessons by a Miss Corbett. The picture which remains in my mind is of her in tweed skirt, brogues and beret, running straight-legged across the lawn at Beech House during some cub activity.

One of the tests cubs had to pass was shoe cleaning, and it was Miss Corbett who judged our prowess in this regard. But we had a secret weapon – Thomas the boilerman. He was a kindly, bear-like man with a twinkling eye, who really seemed to enjoy the intrigue when a cub came to him with a pair of shoes to be surreptitiously polished.

When it was my turn, Thomas happily performed the task for me. But as I ran up the boiler room steps with my brightly polished shoes I unwittingly brushed them against the whitewashed wall. On showing them to Miss Corbett she shook her head and pointed at the white mark down the side of one of them. I could not believe it. The ploy should have been a surefire winner, and yet I failed. I never did pass that shoe-cleaning test, but there was a lesson in there somewhere.

Miss Corbett was a good sport; a plummy, jolly hockey-sticks type, whom I would describe as being distantly likeable. However, she did something to me I didn't appreciate at all.

I'm left-handed, and Miss Corbett believed this could be 'rectified'. She ordered me to use my right hand only, and if I was caught writing left-handed, it was rapped with a wooden ruler. This had quite a bad effect on me. Apart from delaying my ability to write properly by a year or so, the tension brought on a temporary stammer. Apparently King George VI had a stammer caused the same way. It was thought improper for a king to sign documents with his left hand and he was punished for doing it. It didn't work and his stammer remained. I was greatly relieved, after moving out of Miss Corbett's class, to be allowed to revert to my natural left-handedness.

Another side-effect of trying to make me right-handed was that I would get things the wrong way round, like writing the number '9' instead of the letter 'P'. This got to the point where whole words would be written back to front. In one particular essay, for example, I used the word god instead of dog. Hopefully I've been forgiven the blasphemy, and I suspect it made the piece more interesting to read anyway.

This attempt to make me act against my instincts may have been a contributory factor to my bed-wetting, which had plagued me for some time, and if anything increased at Beech House.

I would wake in the mornings not daring to move, because, of course, while lying still and warm it was impossible to know whether the bed was wet. If, on moving, there was the dreaded cold feel of wetness, I was assured of a depressing start to the day. The bed would be stripped and the mattress put out to air, even though it was protected by a rubber sheet, for everyone to see. This was terribly upsetting for me. Only another sufferer can know the ignominy, embarrassment and helplessness of such an affliction.

The good side to this, if it's possible to have a good side to bed-wetting, was that I was not alone. There were four of us, and we were all put together in the same dormitory. Knowing there were fellow sufferers was a comfort. And fortunately we were quite strong characters, good at sport and well liked, so this protected us from the sort of ribbing normally meted out to bed-wetting boys.

Every effort was made to help us. The staff tried not letting us drink after tea-time, and they woke us in the middle of the night to go to the loo. Mr Lewis – or Pa Louie as we called him – had read somewhere that wetting the bed only occurred while lying on the back. So an intricate, Heath Robinson like device was cobbled together to prevent this. It was a harness made of white fabric tape with cotton reels threaded to it. The idea was that the reels would wake us if we turned in our sleep.

Despite the discomfort of these modern-day instruments of torture we still managed to shrug them off in our sleep. In the morning we would be found fast asleep, on our backs, more often than not in a damp patch. Within a week the harnesses were abandoned. Eventually, thank God, nature proved the best cure and we all grew out of bed-wetting. In my case, at around the age of ten.

My sexual education, albeit in a rudimentary form, also began at Rydal.

Every Sunday afternoon we would be taken for a walk in crocodile fashion, each of us paired with another boy. I cannot remember the name of the boy I was with on the particular Sunday I have in mind, but I set off in total innocence and returned with a crude understanding of the basics of human sexual intercourse. Plus one or two extra bits of embellishment. Such as, if your mother limped in the morning it was because she had done 'it' the night before.

I was not totally convinced about all this. I had a problem with the mechanics, and couldn't quite work out how all the parts fitted together. But it was a start.

No formal sex instruction was given to me either by my parents or the school. That was supposed to be picked up as life went along, and experience gained by trial and, mainly, error.

On one occasion, however, my mother did make a fleeting and abortive attempt to find out if I had any knowledge on the subject. We were watching a film called *The Brothers* at our local cinema, the Kings, in which Patricia Roc was being seduced by a Scottish fisherman on the seashore.

After some fully-clothed, and by today's standards fairly chaste, petting, the camera panned sideways on to the sand. Into the empty frame fell Patricia Roc's open hand. The fingers started to close, the grip tightened, harder and harder, the clenched fist rose slightly in ecstasy, and then collapsed, limp.

'What did that mean?' my mother asked.

'I don't know,' I retorted curtly, wishing the camera had stayed where it should have been.

No further enquiry was made, and as no attempt whatsoever to explain was forthcoming, it was other children who provided my sole source of information on the subject.

I suppose it would have been around the age of nine or ten that masturbation was added to our list of hobbies. It was looked upon with no more or less interest than philately or model-making. There was no end result, however, as we were not mature. It was just a pleasurable act with no real sexual connotation or need for a partner.

One boy, who was more advanced than the rest of us, needing to shave while still in junior school, said that he produced some 'stuff' when he did it. We were curious about this phenomenon and said we'd like to see it. He agreed, and one afternoon during playtime a small group of us went behind some screens in the annex garage. He did it and we inspected the content of his hand. This was our first sighting of the male fluid, the great giver of life – and as such we didn't find it particularly impressive. The arrival of my own, however, two years later, was *terribly* impressive and interesting.

In a bizarre kind of way this awakening of sexual awareness tied in with an 'official' hobby that gripped the whole school for some months – collecting the wrappers from chewing gum and chocolate bars thrown down by American GIs stationed nearby. We would stick these in scrap albums and vie with each other as to who had the best collection. On seeing an American soldier the familiar cry of, 'Got any gum, chum?' was just as much for the wrapper as its contents.

One day, a small group gathered around a boy who had found an unusual square packet, the like of which we had never seen before. Our collective and considered opinion was that it was chewing gum. Very quickly, news spread around the school that a new brand of gum had been discovered with the name Durex.

Considering it was wartime, the food at Rydal was pretty good; mainly, I think, because schools were given priority. Breakfast consisted of porridge or cornflakes, fried bread, fried eggs, tomatoes or bacon. Sometimes an enormous baking tray was brought round containing any left-over fried foods, and those who had finished – but only those who had finished – could have seconds. When this tray appeared, anything left on our plates was immediately whipped off and placed either on our knees or into a pocket. There was hardly a boy in the school without a large grease mark on the leg of his grey shorts.

One day, in the classroom, I put my hand into my blazer pocket and felt the soft smoothness of a broken fried egg. I was pleased I never went for seconds of fried tomatoes.

Some foods, sweets in particular, were very scarce, and some were hardly seen at all, like bananas or anything else that had to be shipped in from abroad. One boy, Glover, who had lived in India for a few years with his father, told us he had eaten so many bananas there that he could never face another one. We suspected this may have been exaggerating things somewhat.

When, amid much curiosity and excitement, a consignment of bananas arrived, Glover was put to the test. After supper, each of us was served with one whole banana. It was with a mixture of greed, satisfaction and pity that we watched a crestfallen Glover cut his into slices and hand them round, leaving none for himself.

There was a room on the second floor at Beech House which contained rationed foods. It was strictly out of bounds. But we would post a lookout and take it in turns to creep in and help ourselves to one or two lumps of sugar or a piece of dried fruit. As long as we didn't get too greedy, it was an exciting piece of naughtiness. We did not consider it to be stealing, we saw it as being more like scrumping, and as most of us were involved it was considered a fair sport.

Until someone got carried away, that is.

The first we knew about it was one Saturday afternoon when a full house-assembly was called in the billiards room. There were about forty boys all together, but it was a big room and could accommodate us all. These unscheduled assemblies were rare and heralded an announcement of some importance. So it was with a mixture of elation and trepidation that we filed in and took our seats. When Mr Lewis arrived the expression on his face said it all – it was obviously a matter of some gravity. There was a long, frosty pause before he spoke.

'I am appalled and horrified,' he began. 'There is a thief in the school.'

We sat in nervous anticipation, waiting for him to continue.

'I don't expect to find stealing at all in a school like this, but stealing of the worst kind has taken place. In case you had forgotten, there is a war going on, and people all over the world are starving. In some countries, people are shot for taking food that isn't theirs.'

Guilt was written on every face.

'Someone has been into the food store and stolen a box of raisins,' he went on. 'I know it's one of you and I intend to find out who.'

I blushed, and thought, if he looks at me he'll think I did it.

'I will give the boy responsible a chance to do the honourable thing and own up,' Mr Lewis announced.

After a very long wait, during which no one stirred, he said, 'I'm going up to my study. You will all remain here until the thief comes to me and admits his guilt.'

Then he swept out of the room.

No one spoke for ages. We were all guilty of taking food from the store, but not to that extent. 'Does anyone know who did it?' somebody whispered. No response. We waited and waited. 'I want to go to the bog,' a small voice wailed.

Saturday afternoons were usually spent playing in the garden, climbing trees, building dens and running around in gangs, but all we could do was sit there glumly. Five minutes is a long time at that age, and I can still remember the agony of the *two hour* wait. One boy even offered to own up just to get us out of there, but he didn't. Neither did the real culprit own up.

When Mr Lewis finally came back he said, 'You will all assemble in here after lunch every day until the boy responsible owns up. You may go.'

We shuffled off to bed convinced we would spend the rest of our lives sitting in the billiards room.

But the next morning brought an end to the affair.

We were told to assemble in the billiards room immediately after breakfast, and Mr Lewis, grim faced, was waiting for us. When we settled down he said, 'Stand up, Aspin.'

The boy in question, turning ghastly white before our eyes, slowly rose.

'Do you deny it was you who stole the raisins?'

'No, sir.'

'Why didn't you have the courage to say so?'

Aspin could only manage an almost inaudible whisper, 'I'm sorry, sir.'

'I was considering expulsion for the boy responsible,' the head explained, 'but have decided on a caning. You will all remain here while this is done. Go up to my study, Aspin!'

Head bowed, the wretched boy crept from the room with Mr Lewis close behind.

It seems Aspin had gone to the food store on his own and, unable to resist the temptation, had taken the full box of raisins. Later, in the bog – not a very attractive name for the loo, but that's what it was called – he had eaten the lot. Unfortunately for him, his bowels were not up to it, and so during the night, in his bed, the evidence, so to speak, was revealed.

That evening he showed us the weals from his caning. There had only been four strokes, but each left a raised, blue mark, and one had broken the skin. He had also been caught on the arm when he moved to protect himself and deflected the blow to the back of his leg. Mr Lewis was the kindest of the masters, and caned infrequently, but he was the most feared.

Caning was a part of school life until a new, liberal headmaster, Donald Hughes, had it banned two or three years after I arrived at the senior school. Before that, I only experienced it twice.

The first time was not a caning but a slippering, administered by a dear old man known as Doc Turner, or 'Toc H'. After lights out, at 7 p.m., we were not allowed to talk or get out of bed, except to go to the bog – sorry, loo. On light summer evenings this was particularly hard and we would often leave our beds to look out the window and talk in whispers. A duty master patrolled the dormitories and one night he caught me out of bed twice. After the second time, I was lying in bed with my back to the door, which was at the end of a small recess.

Crawling under the blankets to the bottom of my bed I shouted, 'What do you think I am?' Strangely there was no reply. 'I'm a snail!' I shrieked, sticking my head out from under the bedclothes. 'Well then, you can crawl up to Mr Turner's room, Roache!' a voice boomed. I turned to see the duty master standing in the recess. He had opened and closed the door but remained on the inside. That wasn't really fair play, I thought, but I was well and truly caught.

Up in Mr Turner's room he asked me what I had been doing. 'Playing snails, sir,' I said.

'Incessant talking and getting out of bed is what I hear,' he countered, drawing back a curtain covering a small alcove to reveal a large pile of old slippers. He took one, bent it, smacked it into his other hand, bent it again, then put it back. This process was repeated many times while he delivered a well worn lecture on good behaviour and the need for quiet after lights out. Eventually finding a slipper to his satisfaction, he told me to drop my pyjamas and bend over. He then proceeded to smack me while continuing the lecture between whacks.

On the way back to the dormitory I slipped on the uncarpeted stairs and bounced down a few steps on my bottom and that, other than the interminable lecture, was the most painful part of the incident.

The second occasion was a few years later when I was sleeping in Beech House's annex. We were all in our pyjamas waiting for lights out and I was doing some final adjustments to a model aircraft I had been building. Then I realised that a vital component, the glue, was over in the locker room in the main building. *Sans* slippers and dressing-gown, I dashed down the stairs, across the garden and drive, into the locker room, found my glue and scooted back.

In this fleeting moment lights-out had taken place and a teacher called Josh Howard was standing in my dormitory wondering where the devil I was. Guilty on many counts, and with no defence, I was marched to his room to be caned. It was quick and fairly painless, but it left me feeling humiliated and with a sense that I had not really done anything particularly wrong.

Children are not very sympathetic to infirmity, and Josh Howard's deafness, and his grotesquely inefficient hearing-aid, was a source of great amusement to us. The most popular game in class was to put up a hand with a pencil in it and say, 'Please may I leave the room, sir?' His reply was invariably, 'Yes, do it in the waste-paper basket.'

Another wheeze, but one that took a fair amount of courage, was to approach his desk and mouth something without actually speaking. He would say, 'Just a minute,' and turn up his hearing-aid. The boy would then mime the words again, more energetically, and Josh would turn up the deaf-aid louder still. When it was up to full volume the boy would shout, 'Your deaf-aid is whistling, sir!' This would make him jump, and exclaim, 'All right, all right, don't shout, I can hear you.' This performance always had us rocking with suppressed laughter.

My time in junior school was reasonably happy, although I never quite got over my dread of the first day of a new term. The last evening of the holidays was always celebrated by going to the cinema. But frequently the enjoyment of the film was spoiled by the realisation of what the next day would bring.

I can still feel nervous about Monday mornings.

Something like panic set in as the time to enter the senior school drew near. Leaving the known for the vast unknown was a daunting prospect.

The senior school was separate from Beech House and was requisitioned by the Ministry of Food. Its new home was Oakwood Park, once an hotel, nestling in the hills above Conway.

Oakwood Park was a charming place, surrounded by its own golf course, with grounds which extended well into the open countryside beyond. By the time I arrived the course had been turned over to food production and playing fields. However, it was still possible to imagine slim, elegant people consuming slim, elegant drinks at Oakwood Park's cocktail bar during the hotel's heyday in the 1920s.

I was to spend two years there before returning to the main building at Colwyn Bay to finish my education.

The senior school had a completely different feel to Rydal junior. The masters wore black gowns and mortar boards, and responsibility for discipline was mostly in the hands of prefects, who were eighteen-year-old men. Nevertheless we had much more freedom compared to the junior school and were generally left to our own devices.

But one inflexible rule was that we had to have some kind of hobby to fill the hours between 6.00 and 8.00 p.m. on Monday evenings. So on the first day of that new term my friend Tuckey and I scoured the list of choices pinned outside the school hall. Being a bit lazy by nature, I was looking for the least demanding option. Pastimes on offer included bridge, chess, golf, woodwork, debating, printing, music and gymnastics, none of which greatly appealed.

Then I noticed a small group of boys lounging about on benches in the hall. Some were reading comics, others were staring idly into space. This looked promising. I had not the faintest idea what they were supposed to be doing, but when Tuckey said, 'I'm going in *there*,' the decision was made. We joined them.

The loungers were junior and middle school boys. Over in the main body of the hall a master was arguing with a number of senior boys. A few moments later the seniors walked out on him. He came over, looked us up and down with an obvious lack of enthusiasm and announced despondently, 'It seems you lot are all that's left of the school Dramatic Society.'

Thus was taken the first step on the road to my true vocation.

Dick Tuckey and myself went on to become leading lights in the Dramatic Society, our high point being a half-term production of *Macbeth*, with Tuckey playing the title role and yours truly as Lady Macbeth.

My mother, who was busy directing productions for Ilkeston Town Womens Guild at the time, was delighted. But after seeing plays I was in, instead of the usual proud parent's, 'well done', she would hand me notes on how to improve my performance. This was very valuable, and I'm sure it contributed to my winning the school drama cup when I appeared in Ibsen's *Enemy of the People*.

Tuckey was very bright and academic. He wrote a play in verse while we were at school, and set himself the task of reading the Bible from beginning to end. He was offered a good place at Cambridge, but preferred to go to Bristol Old Vic drama school with a view to entering the acting profession. This he did and has been a very successful artistic director of a number of theatres including the Belgrade at Coventry and the Liverpool Playhouse.

One of the disappointments of my life is that I lack musical talent. I would love to be able to play an instrument well, and to sing. Indeed it's become a standing joke with the cast of *Coronation Street* that my singing is characterised by its constantly changing key. Barbara Knox, who is a good singer, often says, 'Don't sing, Bill.' Or, if she wants a laugh, 'Do sing, Bill.'

There are three kinds of shop windows that still really thrill me. One is a window filled with sweets and another is one filled with woodwork tools. But the most exciting of all is the window of a shop selling musical instruments.

Therefore, it was natural, when I reached senior school, that I should request music tuition. For a year I took piano lessons with Percy Haywood, the music master, and advanced to being able to read simple chords. At which point I transferred my affections to the trumpet.

Maybe it is an echo of a previous life, but whenever I hear the sound of a trumpet or bugle I could almost burst with excitement. The first time I was aware of this was in junior school, when we played cricket against the naval college side from HMS Conway. After the game we boarded the old ship, which was moored in the Menai Straight, for tea and a tour. Before we left, a bugler sounded the last post, and it stirred something deep inside me.

Another teacher was found to give me trumpet lessons. At our preliminary meeting – from which I believe he gathered that my lack of ability was compensated for by enthusiasm – he warned me that some people were physically unsuited to play the instrument. But he promised to bring a trumpet to our next meeting and, if all was well, I could buy it for fifteen pounds.

I spent the interim terrified I would be physically unsuitable, and regularly examined my lips and teeth for any minor abnormalities. But apart from one tooth in my lower jaw being out of line, due to a blow from a hockey stick, all seemed in order.

By the time of our second appointment my nerves were shredded from worrying about whether I would pass the 'physical'. When I arrived the tutor was there with a black leather case and a music stand. He opened the case and there it was – a silver Boosey and Hawkes trumpet. I had never seen anything more magnificent.

He explained about putting my lips and tongue together and almost dry spitting into the mouthpiece. I did this for a while until I got a consistent sound. Then he attached the mouthpiece to the trumpet, showed me how to hold it correctly, and handed it to me. I still recall the joy of holding that sacred instrument for the first time. I was enchanted.

I was then taught the valve positions and, the half-hour up, how the trumpet went back into its case. The instrument duly purchased – I had convinced mother that my very life depended on having it – he bid me good day and told me to be back at the same time the following week. And not a mention of physical unsuitability.

I picked up the case, walked out of the school and made my way up Pwllycrochan Avenue, into the woods overlooking Colwyn Bay. I found an area off the main path hidden by bushes and sat down with the case on my knee. I took out the trumpet and held it, relishing the fact that it was mine.

That trumpet was played at every opportunity. Slow tunes like 'Shenendoah' and 'Red River Valley', and carols and hymns, were favourites. My big hero, of course, was 'the man with the golden trumpet', Eddie Calvert. I tried all the Al Jolson songs – 'California. Here I Come', 'Mammy', 'Climb Upon My Knee, Sonny Boy', 'Baby Face' – and played until I lost all feeling in my lips. I also played 'Jerusalem' in the school music competition.

The neighbours around Rutland House always knew when I was home on holiday. All the hours I blasted away should have turned me into a Louis Armstrong or a Harry James, but the only improvement was that I could play for longer. Although I imagine the neighbours would have argued with the word improvement.

Years later, in *Coronation Street,* I had the opportunity, as Ken Barlow, to play my trumpet for an audience of sixteen million people. Both occasions were Christmas concerts, the first in Ena Sharples' mission hall, the second when Ernie Bishop (Stephen Hancock) formed a band. The line-up consisted of Ernie on piano, Billy Walker (Ken Farrington) and myself on trumpets, and Alan Howard (Alan Browning) on the guitar. We played 'Yellow Bird'. Or perhaps 'murdered' would be a more appropriate way of putting it.

My wonderful silver trumpet was exchanged at some stage for an inferior brass one, which I still have in the loft at home. From time to time my children get it out and make noises on it. In fact Verity, my daughter, has just asked if she can have lessons. But whatever fire it was that burned in me is now extinguished, and I no longer have the desire to play. I still have ambitions to sing though, heaven help us.

My arrival back at the main school in Colwyn Bay, where my education was completed, coincided with the appointment of a new headmaster, the aforementioned Donald Hughes.

Mr Hughes was a tall, slim man with a glass eye. He was sensitive by nature and liberal by inclination. One of his first acts was to abolish corporal punishment and instigate fireside chats for miscreants. This was all very well, but for some reason I was cast as one of the miscreants; indeed, I was regarded as their leader.

This surprised me as I have always thought of myself as quiet, retiring, polite and unwilling to offend. However it's only fair to say these attributes go hand in hand with an independent way of thinking, a love of freedom, and respect for justice rather than the law. My feeling is that when rules are man-made they are *per se* inadequate and need continual refinement. This philosophy, which was not rationally conceived, did not lead me into serious trouble so much as a steady drip of minor offences.

Donald Hughes called me in for one of his fireside chats after a conflict between myself and the head prefect. Several of us had been gated (forbidden to go out) for two hours on a Saturday afternoon because of an accumulation of minor transgressions during the week. We were given the task of shifting a pile of sand on New Field, the main sports ground, to a more convenient place. Just as the time was up, the head prefect came along and said we had to finish the job. I said the two hours were now over. There was an impasse and he reported me. Hence the chat.

Going to the headmaster's study is always daunting and I was very nervous as I approached his door. On entering, the head invited me to sit in an armchair by the fire, and pressed a bell to summon the housekeeper. He asked her for tea and biscuits for two, and to tell the head prefect to pop in.

In due course the head prefect arrived, gave his side of the story and left. Then, over tea, Mr Hughes solicited my views on discipline. How would I have handled the incident? What did I think of corporal punishment? It was all very civilised and we talked for about half an hour with no further mention of my dispute with the prefect.

I came away from the headmaster's study with a great respect and liking for him, and an unspoken endorsement of my attitude to discipline and rules.

Donald Hughes was always approachable, the epitome of fairness and kindness, while maintaining the authority and dignity of his position. Not long after I left Rydal he was involved in a bad car accident. He was making a good recovery in hospital when tragically, just before being discharged, he had a heart attack and died. It was a sad and premature end for a good, dear man.

During my time at Rydal my passion for cinema was well and truly established. Every Saturday night in the winter term a film would be shown in the school hall, with the projector manned by the redoubtable Dr Britten, the physics master.

The fare consisted almost entirely of movies made in the 1930s, and I still enjoy them when they come on television. Will Hay, Old Mother Riley, Abbott and Costello, Laurel and Hardy, early Hitchcock's and *The Scarlet Pimpernel*, with Leslie Howerd, were particular favourites. I loved those Saturday night film shows.

The greater freedom afforded to sixth-formers meant my friends and I could nip out to the matinées in Colwyn Bay's cinemas most afternoons. This was in fact forbidden – we were only supposed to go to the cinema four times a term by special pass – but we were never caught. I saw more films in my last two years at school than all the years since.

I was very influenced by this heavy cinematic diet, and the film that made the greatest impact on me was *The Jolson Story*. It's by no means a great film, but it excited me enormously. The story of this born showman, a man who could entertain and knew it, who broke with his family background and overcame all obstacles to achieve his aims, hit a pulse in me. It harmonised totally with whatever it was that made me want to become an actor.

All this cinema-going made quite a dent in our pocket money, and we would often resort to a naughty trick. Pooling enough pennies for a single ticket, one of us went in and, under the pretext of using the loo, opened the fire-door for the rest of us. Anyone watching must have been suspicious to see one boy go into the loo and six come out, but amazingly we were never caught.

There were two sets of houses at Rydal, the sports houses and the sleeping houses. The sports houses were Corinthians, Crusaders, Trojans and Barbarians. Needless to say, I was a Barbarian. The sleeping houses were New house, Old house, Ingleside, Beech and Walshaw. I was in Ingleside.

Ingleside's housemaster was Donald Boumphrey, and the Matron was Gertie Senior. Boumphrey, or Bunch as we called him, was something of a character. He was a short, thickset man with strong, rough hands, a round, weather-beaten face and shapeless nose. Bunch always had an unlit pipe in his mouth and made a 'tschll' sucking noise when he talked. He was much imitated because of this.

He taught latin, but his real interests were the school cricket and rugby teams. One of Bunch's characteristics was his tendency to fall asleep during his lessons, and this was the only time the class could be guaranteed to be totally silent. Then a 'tschll' and the lifting of his head would indicate he was back again.

A test in Bunch's class would go like this: 'Tschll. Open your exercise books. We are, tschll, having a test. Right, the first question is, what is the latin for "night", tschll?' Then his head would slowly sink forward and in no time he was asleep. We would write *nox*, if we knew it, or even look up our latin primer if we wanted to, but none of this was necessary. Because after a few minutes he would lift his head and say, 'Tschll. The answer is *nox*. Tick it if you've got it right.' (Which we did, or wrote it in if we had not.) 'The next one is "farmer", tschll.' And back he'd go to the land of nod.

He just wanted to sail along avoiding trouble and thinking about his beloved cricket and rugby. He was a man of very few words, totally at a loss in female company. Or indeed in any company.

The only way he could indicate warmth or kindness to a boy was by calling him 'a bloody fool'. One boy in our dormitory, Thirlby, managed to smuggle in a large cake his mother had made for him and we decided to hold a midnight feast. After lights out we sat in a circle on the dormitory floor and the provider of the cake began to cut it into slices. Suddenly, to our surprise and horror, the door opened and there stood Bunch. After what seemed an age he said, 'What the devil's going on here, tschll?' Thirlby said, 'We're having some cake, sir. Would you like a piece?' The silence that followed was greater than those in his latin classes as we waited for the expected explosion. Eventually he said, 'You bloody fool, Thirlby,' and left us to finish our cake.

The Matron, Gertie Senior, was also a bit of a character.

She would roll her eyes heavenward and adopt a long-suffering smile at the mere mention of Mr Boumphrey. But I'm sure that in their own way they were really rather fond of each other.

Gertie was amusing and approachable. She was the centre of information and gossip about the doings and whereabouts of all the Old Boys. She appeared on my *This is Your Life*, and it was delightful to meet her again, and to see she had not changed in the thirty years or so that had passed. She's still going strong in Colwyn Bay, but is long retired from Rydal, of course.

I once summoned up the courage to ask a girl called Gwendoline, one of Beech House's maids, to meet me behind the school pavilion. We spent the entire time we were there talking about when we could see each other again. And our liaison was not made any easier by the knowledge that two of my so called friends were giggling in the bushes nearby. I never did 'date' Gwendoline again, but she always gave me a nice smile when we passed in the corridors. This was probably one of the big missed opportunities in my life.

The object of everyone's lust, however, was Nurse Taylor, who ran the school sanatorium. There were an unusually high number of strained thighs on the rugby field in need of massage during her term of office. And I don't think she was unaware of or displeased by the attention she got.

My happiness knew no bounds when a boy once told me that on seeing me walk past, Nurse Taylor had commented, 'Roache is quite a good-looking boy in a hawkish sort of way.' Later, still unmarried, she became the Matron of New House, causing an avalanche of applications from boys to transfer from other houses.

I enjoyed my last year in the sixth form. I was a prefect and head of house and we spent our study periods playing Canasta.

In my last year in the sixth-form I was taking biology, physics and chemistry, as I was supposed to be going on to study medicine at St Bartholomew's like my father and grandfather. That was a shame because my best subjects, and the ones I enjoyed most, were English, history and scripture. I was in fact better qualified to become a vicar than a doctor. Chemistry and physics I particularly disliked but I did enjoy biology.

Biology was taught by Mrs Olive James, a delightful woman who I think was a war widow, and she took me for extra biology at her house in Llandudno. I liked Mrs James and I know she liked me – possibly this was another of life's missed opportunities. I look back with happiness on my relationship with her.

I passed well in biology, no doubt as a result of my extra tuition with Mrs James, but not in physics and chemistry. Consequently, there was no immediate place for me at St Bartholomew's. And National Service beckoned.

Indeed, I never had the experience of actually leaving school, as I went into the holidays expecting to return to retake physics and chemistry, but received my call-up papers a few weeks later. It was assumed I would continue the studies necessary for a life in medicine after National Service.

But I already had other ideas.

Three

I registered for the Army while still at Rydal, so I knew I would be in one of the regiments of the Welsh Brigade, all of which were serving in Korea.

The idea of fighting in the Korean war generated a chill of fear in the pit of my stomach. But alongside that was a small tingle of excited anticipation at the thought of such an adventure.

I was to be a member of the Royal Welch Fusiliers, and was told to report to Hightown Barracks, Wrexham by 1600 hours on Thursday, 3rd January, 1952.

My parents drove me to Derby station to catch a midday train. Standing on the platform, clutching the tiny suitcase of personal items I was allowed, I said goodbye with all the conviction of a condemned man. I had no idea what to expect from Army life, and feared bullying, theft and violence. Consequently I left my watch and fountain pen at home and carried only a small amount of cash.

There was a duty sergeant and two other uniformed men at Wrexham station, obviously on the lookout for anyone needing a lift to the barracks. The new conscripts were easily recognisable: nervous, white-faced eighteen-year-olds with suitcases. Just like me. The sergeant approached them as they left the station and pointed to a three-ton lorry, in the back of which a few dejected characters were already seated.

Wanting to commit myself in my own time, I slipped into the buffet, and sat drinking tea as the truck rolled off with its crestfallen load. After relaxing for a while I left the station and asked directions to the barracks. As I still had two hours to spare I decided to walk and make the most of my last taste of freedom.

At 3.45 p.m. I passed through the gates of Hightown Barracks. From now on I would be known as 22626311 Fusilier Roache.

I was directed to the gymnasium, where I found about half a dozen other new arrivals being addressed by an elderly major, who looked as though he was probably on the verge of retirement. He came over and welcomed me to the Army. There was no shaking of hands, but his attitude was kindly. He asked if there was anything I wanted to know.

Before I could answer, a sergeant, bristling with energy, bounced in. He saluted the major, who promptly departed, never to be seen again. Then the sergeant turned to us and bellowed, 'Right, you horrible lot! Outside!'

This was my *real* introduction to the Army.

We hefted our suitcases and shambled after him. He formed us into pairs and shouted, 'From now on you do everything at the double! That means you *run*! Follow me!' We set off at a fast trot behind him, going around, not on, the square. I later discovered the square was a sacred place, reserved for drill and ceremonials only, and you transgressed this rule at your peril.

The barrack block was on two floors with two barrack rooms on each. Ours was the left-hand one on the ground floor. This was a long linoleum-floored dormitory with twelve iron beds, six on either side, each with its own tall locker.

'Put your cases on a bed and fall in outside!' came the now familiar roar. I dropped my case on a central bed on the side opposite the windows, picking with random casualness the place that was to be my home, my base, my retreat for the next six weeks.

'This is Ellis Block,' the sergeant informed us, 'in case you get lost. We will now get you kitted out. At the double!'

Over in the stores we were loaded with blankets, sheets and pillows. Holding these in front of us we took them, at the double, to our barrack room. Then, at the double, it was back to the stores, where we were issued with two battledresses, an overcoat, beret, steel helmet, long woollen underwear, socks, shirts, housewife, a tie, knife, fork, spoon, mug, mess tins, kitbag and the two pairs of black boots with which we were to have a love/hate relationship over the coming weeks. A housewife, I should explain, is a canvas roll-up containing needles, cotton, darning wool and spare buttons.

As much of this as possible was crammed into the kitbag, the rest placed over it, then – at the double, naturally – we staggered to our barrack room once more. If we thought we were going to be allowed a breather at this point we were sadly mistaken. The inevitable cry of, 'Fall in outside!' sounded yet again, and we were off to a different store. This time we had a small pack, a large pack, assorted pieces of webbing, a pull-through and a bottle of oil slapped into our arms. Then we were handed a .303 Enfield rifle complete with bayonet.

This brought home to us that we really were in the Army.

That first evening, apart from a break to go to the cookhouse for our first taste of Army food, was spent familiarising ourselves with the kit. We were taught how to fold it and put it away in our lockers, how to make and unmake our beds, square-off our blankets, lay out our areas and, hardest of all, how to bull-up – highly polish – a pair of boots for the morning. By lights-out at 11 o'clock we were only too ready to collapse on to our unyielding beds.

It seemed I had hardly closed my eyes when a bugle sounded and an NCO was walking down the barrack room hitting the end of our beds with a pick handle and shouting, 'Come on, you idle lot! Hands off cocks, on socks!' Unbelievably, it was reveille. Six-thirty on a dark, cold January morning.

We abluted, struggled into battledress and boots, picked up mug, knife, fork and spoon, and marched to the cookhouse for breakfast. After that, we had to make our beds, place knife, fork and spoon square around the mug with its handle pointing to the middle of the room, bump and polish the floor and wait for the platoon sergeant's inspection.

The sergeant did not so much enter as suddenly appear, as if shot up through the floor like a pantomime genie.

'Stand by your beds!' he ordered. 'You don't know what attention is yet, but you soon will. Feet together, hands straight down your sides. Look straight ahead. If I talk to you, you do not look at me. You look straight ahead. And you call me Sergeant at all times. Is that understood?'

There were a few ragged 'yeahs' and 'yeses', then:

'Is that understood?'

'Yes!'

'And you call me sergeant at all times!'

'Yes, sergeant!'

'That's better.'

He walked to the first bed. 'These blankets aren't square,' he said, flinging them off, 'and that webbing's all wrong. Everything is folded badly.'

The platoon sergeant said virtually the same thing to all of us.

On reaching the door he turned and shouted, 'I have never seen such a horrible mess outside of a shithouse! You're a load of wankers! I'll give you ten minutes to get everything back in good order! Then fall in on the square for your first drill lesson! I can see there's a lot of work to be done on you miserable lot!'

We did our best then dashed out to the square. 'I have never seen such a rotten shower in all my life!' the sergeant balled. I must admit we did look a sight, with our berets sticking out sideways, the adjusting ribbons dangling down our backs, webbing belts either too loose or too tight and gaiters on back to front or upside down.

'You're all confined to barracks for six weeks,' he barked. 'We don't want a rabble like you walking around town. I'm going to make you look like soldiers, march like soldiers and bloody well *be* soldiers. Though, God help me, you are the most pathetic lot I have ever had the misfortune to meet. You all look as if the best part of you ran down your mothers' legs!'

I was already getting used to the verbal abuse which, strangely, was not offensive. It was as if they were playing a part and this was just the dialogue they had to use.

What affected me far more was the language of my fellow fusiliers. I did not consider myself a prude, and was not above using the odd furtive four-letter word, but this in no way prepared me for the tidal wave of obscenities my fellow conscriptees employed as a matter of course.

It didn't shock me – well, to be honest, it did a little at first – it more amazed and surprised me. I recall how, on that first evening when we were all wrestling with our unfamiliar kit, one fusilier strolled over to his friend, whose bed was next to mine, and asked if he would like to go for a walk. That was the gist of it anyway. What he actually said was, 'I'm fucked. I'm fucking going for a bastard walk. Are you fucking coming, you cunt?' If this was normal conversation I wondered what they said when they really *needed* to swear. But after a few days I grew accustomed to it.

During those first days of drill we were taught how to fall in, in three ranks, stand to attention, stand at ease, march with a straight back and straight arms, to turn to the right and turn to the left. The main effect of this was to give us all blisters, and our boots became instruments of agony. But very soon they transformed into the most comfortable footwear imaginable. The big dread throughout an Army career is having to break in a new pair of boots.

Finally Sunday came along, which was a free day, but we weren't allowed to leave the barracks. At least this gave us the opportunity to talk and get to know each other.

The fusilier with the bed on my left was a farm labourer called Mathias. While I sat on my bed writing a letter home I was aware of him watching me keenly. When I finished he came over and somewhat deferentially asked if I would complete the crossword in his paper. He was, it turned out, illiterate, and had convinced himself we would win the crossword prize money because I could write.

Another discovery was that the two fusiliers at the top end of the barracks, who kept very much to themselves, were Eton lads. We were a pretty varied cross-section.

By the following week the difference in our appearance and behaviour was truly amazing. Our berets were pulled neatly down at one side, with no sign of the ribbons at the back, and we looked as if we'd had them for years. This was due to having discovered the trick of soaking them in water and jumping on them a lot. We were marching smartly, drilling well with the rifles and saluting every officer in sight with great zeal.

As we came near to finishing our six weeks of basic training some hint of our future was revealed. Being allowed out of barracks when off duty, and perhaps even our first thirty-six hour passes and a home visit, were in prospect. After that we would be posted to Brecon, South Wales, for advanced training before a posting to Korea.

In the meantime, training, and the slow conversion from schoolboys to fusiliers, continued.

One morning, as we were preparing for kit inspection, a corporal came in with a clipboard and said he wanted to know about our educations. Going up to the first man, he said, 'Have you got any educational qualifications, fusilier?'

'What's that, Corporal?'

'Well, have you got a school certificate?'

'Oh no, Corporal.'

And so on down the line, garnering only 'no's', until he came to me.

'Have you got a school certificate?'

'Yes, Corporal, and a higher certificate in Botany and Zoology.' He hesitated for a moment, obviously tremendously impressed with the school certificate. Then he made a note on his clipboard and moved on.

When he reached the last man and repeated the familiar query, the reply was, 'Well actually, Corporal, I've got an honours degree in English and History from Cambridge.'

'Don't try to get out of it!' the corporal snapped. 'Have you got a school certificate?'

There was no answer to that.

Probably two or three times a day I would stamp to attention and identify myself to a superior officer as, '22626311 Fusilier Roache, sir!' This recitation of number rank and name quickly became second nature.

I remember Fred Feast, who played Fred Gee in *Coronation Street*, asking me a few years ago if I could remember my Army number. Without hesitation I said, '22626311'. 'Right,' he said, 'now give me your officers' number.' I hadn't a clue. The only time I would have needed that was if I'd become a prisoner of war. I knew it began with a four but that was all.

It will come as no great surprise to you that a large proportion of the men in the Royal Welch Fusiliers were called Jones. They were differentiated by the use of the last two digits of their number. So 22626335 Jones, for example, was simply known as '35'. These were regarded rather like nicknames, and everyone soon became accustomed to them.

This was a little unfortunate as far as 22626300 Jones was concerned. He became 'fuck all'. But he sportingly responded to this without rancour or any trace of embarrassment.

*　　*　　*

The end of basic training was marked by a passing out parade before our commanding officer. Even before this we were beginning to feel like old campaigners, as since our arrival there had been two further intakes of new recruits. We felt like seasoned veterans as we watched them going through those first awful days.

Our platoon acquitted itself well enough at the passing-out parade to be chosen as the guard of honour for the regimental colours on a march to Wrexham town hall. This was to hear the mayor announce the ascension of the young Queen Elizabeth to the throne.

I was tremendously thrilled by this. With the white feathered hackle in our berets, and the black flash on our backs, we looked magnificent as we marched behind the regimental band. It was wonderful to see people lining the streets to watch us.

We went home on our first leave with heightened confidence and lots of stories to tell. Shortly after our return, we were posted to Dering Lines, Brecon.

Our new home at Brecon was a large wooden hut with a concrete floor. The ventilator at one end had been knocked out, leaving a two-foot square hole through which whisps of snow were blowing, and the only heating was a pot-bellied stove. The brick-built barracks at Wrexham were paradise by comparison. That night we slept in just about every article of clothing we possessed, including our greatcoats.

Next day, in the welcome warmth of the cookhouse, I got a shock when I looked out of the window and saw a mountain. Having arrived in the dark we had no idea of the surrounding terrain, which was of course the Brecon Beacons.

Morning parade was bigger than anything we had experienced before, with three companies on the square, each consisting of about 120 men. Afterwards, everyone was dismissed except us. The Regimental Sergeant Major and a sergeant came over to where we were standing, and the RSM welcomed us.

'This is your platoon sergeant, Sergeant Thomas,' he added. 'He will take you through your advanced training, starting today. Fusiliers Glazebrook, Griffiths and Roache fall out and come to me.'

We took the regulation one step forward, turned to the right, did not salute, as there was no officer on parade, and briskly marched to the RSM.

Sergeant Thomas stamped to attention and screamed, 'Platoon at-ten-SHUN! Riiiight TURN! By the right, quiiiiick MARCH!' Off they went and we hardly saw any of them again, apart from fleetingly in the cookhouse, and finally just before they embarked for Korea. From where two of them never returned.

'Right, lads,' the RSM said. 'You three are to join the Potential Leaders platoon. You'll wear red bands on your epaulets which you will now get from the clothing store. Then report to the commander of B company. Off you go.'

Griffiths and Glazebrook were the Etonians; apparently poor old Jones with the honours degree was thought physically unsuitable to be a potential leader but was later transferred to the Intelligence Corps. We collected our red tabs and reported to the major commanding B company.

The Major was an old soldier who had come up through the ranks and was shortly to retire. Unfortunately there was a bitterness about him, and he left us standing to attention while he spoke. 'You may or may not be officer material, that will be revealed by the War Office Selection Board. Until then you are under *my* command and will be treated no differently to anyone else. Don't think you're going to have a cushy time while you're waiting because you won't. I've got a nice little job lined up for you three – cleaning the latrines and wash-houses. Dismiss.'

We were then taken to the Potential Leaders hut and introduced to the rest of the platoon.

There were about twelve of us in the PL platoon, mostly

ex-public school boys. Some had already taken their War Office Selection Board (WOSBY) examinations and were waiting to be called for officer cadet training. We hungrily devoured every detail of their WOSBY experience. There was a fairly quick turnover in the PL platoon, with two or three leaving at a time, usually to go to Eaton Hall, the Duke of Westminster's home, for officer cadet training. A steady trickle of new arrivals kept the platoon topped up.

Our platoon sergeant was fairly relaxed, as sergeants go, and had a sense of humour. Almost. Each morning we fell in, in front of the company office, and he gave us instructions for the day. One morning he came out and said, 'We've got a nice little treat for you today – a ten-mile march with full kit and rifles.' Peter Glazebrook, standing at the back, said in a small, tired voice, 'Oh dear, Sergeant, must we?' This would normally have caused a sergeant's veins to stand out in his neck and his eyes to bulge, followed by a tirade of abuse and a lecture on what it meant to be in the Army. Sergeant Thomas, however, said, 'Terribly sorry, Glazebrook, but I'm afraid we *must*.' We all roared with laughter, mainly from relief.

Much to my surprise, after two weeks at Dering Lines, and not yet three months into my Army career, I was promoted to lance corporal. All this really did was make me a sort of dormitory monitor, responsible for us all being in the right place at the right time.

My promotion caused me one moment of embarrassment. I was put in charge of a small working-party detailed to mend some barbed-wire fencing. The party was made up of fusiliers waiting to be discharged. Some were old soldiers with twenty years' service who had been through the war. Others were National Servicemen completing their two years, and several had served in Korea.

While we were working, the conversation among the fusiliers was for the most part about where they had been and what they had done. During a lull, an old fusilier, ingrained with respect for authority, asked, 'What have *you* done, Corporal?' I tried to avoid saying, 'basic training'. He followed with, 'Well, how long have you been in the Army?' 'Three months,' I said, lying a little. I can still see the look on his face. *What the hell is the army coming to?* was written all over it.

Although I was not yet too well acquainted with pubs, I found myself in one of Brecon's on a free evening and met a very attractive girl. I blush to confess that I cannot remember her name. I walked her home and arranged to meet her on the following Sunday afternoon. She must have made most of the running as I was still diffident in the company of young females.

Sunday afternoon was a bright April day and we walked by a river and lay down on the grass bank. We talked for a long time, and then I kissed her. She was very receptive. The next meeting was to be arranged by telephone and this was to be made easy by her working at the local telephone exchange. There was a public phone box near the gate of the camp and at six o'clock each evening she would be listening on that line. All I had to do was pick up the phone, tap three times on the cradle, and she would be there. Of course, as fate would have it, the following morning we were informed we would be spending ten days at Cwm Gwdi, the rifle range in the hills, and that evening was to be spent packing our kit.

I was at the telephone box for our 6.00 p.m. chat. I went in, picked up the phone, then thought about how I could break our date without sounding as if I didn't want to see her again. So I practised out loud. 'I'm terribly sorry, but I won't be able to see you for some time . . .' No, no; that really sounded as if I didn't want to see her. 'Erm, I'm afraid I've been posted to Cwm Gwdi, and . . .' No. She wouldn't know what Cwm Gwdi was.

In the middle of these vocal agonies I suddenly became aware of a female Welsh voice saying, 'What are you talking about?' I went scarlet, not having realised she was already listening. I muttered some inept explanation before going into the difficult enough purpose of the call. Not having helped myself with the introduction she didn't sound fully convinced, but nevertheless agreed to meet me on my return.

We did meet on a few more occasions before Army postings intervened and that was the end of that. She was not my first introduction to fumbling sexual activity, but certainly a close second. The first was a girl called Kath, whom I'd met at a New Year's Eve dance in Ilkeston town hall. We were very close friends for several years.

Quite a few weeks elapsed before my summons to the War Office Selection Board came through, and I was growing very nervous about the whole thing. Possibly my entire military career depended on the outcome.

I had gleaned a fair amount of information about WOSBY. I knew it lasted three days, that you were under constant observation and that it included a whole series of tests and examinations, one of which was having to give a fifteen-minute talk.

This all took place at Barton Stacey camp, near Andover, and when I arrived there I found that the Potential Officers quarters were in a separate, self-contained part of the compound. This was made up of several concrete buildings which actually had curtains in the windows. There was a sitting area with cheap carpeting and uniform green easy chairs.

There were ten of us on the course and we were greeted by a small, dapper captain with a moustache, complete with a cane under his arm. His first words were, 'Come in and sit down, gentlemen.' After the forms of address we had grown accustomed to, 'gentlemen' stood out like the Queen at a bag ladies' convention.

'You will find a list on the notice-board of your room allocation and there is also a number by your name,' he explained. 'You will find a patch with this number on the beds in your rooms. Wear it at all times during your stay here. I suggest you now get yourselves settled in. Thank you, gentlemen.'

Yes, we each had our own rooms, which were little more than cubicles, but the bed was made of wood, not iron. There was a small wardrobe, a table and a chair. As promised, on the bed was my number, made of two pieces of cloth about ten inches square, one for the front and one for the back, connected at the top by two straps to go over the shoulders. At the bottom were two further tapes for tying around the waist. For the next three days I was to be number 42.

In our group there were two men from the regular Army, one who had been in the marines for two years, and a sergeant with four years service. All the others, apart from one who had been to university on deferment and got a degree, were straight from school like me.

We gathered in the sitting area at 9.30 the following morning. Two captains arrived carrying clipboards. One of them, who in the event was to do most of the talking, began by saying, 'I want you to relax and enjoy yourselves. We're not here to catch you out, just to find out a little more about you.' This did not make us feel any easier at all.

'To get to know each other better,' he continued, 'I want you to tell us a little about yourselves. Starting with you, number 40.' Number 40 was one of the confident, bright sparks and come over as such. I was really nervous by the time my turn came and was pleasantly surprised to hear my voice coming out strong and clear as I talked about my family, school and sporting interests.

We were then taken to a classroom where we each stood behind a table on which were placed dismantled parts of vehicle engines and given an hour to reassemble them. A bit like *The Krypton Factor*. I had no problem with this as I had already totally stripped down and rebuilt an old motorcycle, and enjoyed this sort of work.

There followed a very demanding timed assault course.

After lunch there was an awful test designed to see who became the natural leader of the group. We stood before a concrete structure about ten-foot square, with an open window and door, and a slot about four-foot square in its roof. On the ground was a dummy on a stretcher.

'Right, gentlemen,' the talkative captain began. 'The dummy is a wounded man unable to leave the stretcher. He is to be taken into the chamber, up through the hole on to the roof, down the outside and back here. Off you go!'

Instant chaos.

Three of the group tried to pick up the front of the stretcher with no one on the back. The rest of us stood around shouting orders which were totally ignored. The dummy fell off the stretcher. Eventually we managed to get the stretcher and dummy into the chamber, but it kept falling off as attempts were made to push it through the roof. Had this been a real wounded individual his injuries would by now have been considerably more serious than when we started.

Amid much shoving and shouting an effort was made to strap the dummy to the stretcher with belts. I jumped on to the roof and attempted to pull the stretcher and dummy through the hole. Several of the others were still yelling themselves hoarse in an attempt to take charge but they were looking more and more ridiculous by the minute.

At the expense of a great deal of chaos and confusion the mission was completed. After a fashion.

We were then given exercises in which we took turns being in charge. I was first. We assembled in front of two trees about fifteen feet apart. 'Number 42,' the captain said, 'between those trees is a deep, fast-flowing river. You have to get all your men, with dry rifles and this rope, on to the other side. Off you go!'

I turned to the rest of the group. 'Who's a strong swimmer?' I asked. No reply. The competitiveness of the situation obviously meant they weren't going to go out of their way to be cooperative. A firm line was called for.

I looked to the marine, feeling on pretty safe ground with him. 'Can you swim?' He could. 'Give your rifle to the man next to you,' I ordered, 'and tie this rope around your waist. Take off your boots, belt and beret and swim across the river. We'll have you on the rope, so you won't be swept away.'

'You,' I indicated to another of my companions. 'Tie the other end of the rope around that tree.' He hurried off to do this and I told the rest of them to put their rifles on their backs. By this time the marine had mimed crossing the 'river'.

'Tie your end of the rope around the tree,' I called over to him. 'The rest of you get in line and cross hand-over-hand.' I felt good about the way it was going. Well, until the end anyway, Because when we were all over, the captain said, 'Well done, 42. But what about the rope?' It was still tied to the tree on the other side. He didn't seem too concerned about this, however, apparently being more interested in how we handled things generally. These individual leadership exercises took us to the end of the first full day.

The second day began with a one-hour group debate on topics of our choosing. Verbal vying was so intense for the first twenty minutes that I couldn't get a word in. Fortunately, somebody repeated something he'd said earlier and I plunged in with, 'We must have exhausted this subject if we're repeating ourselves. Here's a new one – should we have an independent nuclear deterrent?' They were all so desperate to pick up on anything that they piled in with renewed vigour. So far, so good.

This over, we were each given a map, compass and three grid references, put in a lorry and dropped off separately at different points. We had to find our way to the grid references and back to base by lunchtime.

The remainder of the afternoon was taken up with our fifteen-minute talks, followed by a question and answer session. I picked acting as my theme, not that I knew a great deal about it at that stage, but I assumed they wouldn't either. It paid off. Acting didn't really lend itself to hostile cross-examination and I got away with it.

The morning of the third and final day started with a session on the rifle range, followed by us taking it in turns to drill the rest of the group. This was relatively light-hearted as officers are notoriously bad at drill.

The last hurdle was the most awesome – going before the board for final questioning.

These were the men who would decide whether or not I was suitable to be sent on to the Officer Cadet Training Unit (OCTU).

This took place in a large bare room. Immediately opposite the door were three trestle tables placed end to end with Army blankets as tablecloths. Eight officers of varying rank sat behind them. On the left was a blackboard covered with another blanket. I never discovered what was written on it, but assumed it was some sort of memory aid for the committee. Or possibly the final results were chalked up there.

There was no invitation to sit down, nor indeed a chair had I been invited to do so. But this was not an interrogation; the questioning was relaxed and easy, more conversational than testing. I cannot remember much about the questions, except that one officer asked me about corporal punishment. 'Would you be prepared to give an order for someone to receive corporal punishment?' he wanted to know. 'If I felt it was necessary,' I said, 'yes.' I did not go on to say I could hardly think of a case when it would be necessary.

All that remained was an agonising wait for the result.

Some of the group, myself included, were in a terrible state of nerves. Several talked rather too loudly, as if to bolster their confidence. As always when anxious, I just became quieter and quieter.

On the stroke of 3 p.m. the captain came in carrying a

bundle of small white slips. We all knew they would have printed on them:

1   Recommended for officer cadet training
2   Not recommended for officer cadet training
3   Recommended to apply again in six months

and that two of the sentences would be crossed out.

'I hope you've enjoyed your stay with us, gentlemen,' he said. 'As soon as you get your result, pick up your kit and report to the guardroom, where transport will be arranged to take you to the station. Good luck.' He then walked down the line handing out the pieces of paper.

I was towards the end, and watched as each of my fellow hopefuls received their slips. The results weren't in an envelope, or folded, so they could be seen before being handed to you. The suspense, although brief, was almost unbearable.

The first man looked straight back at the captain and then at the rest of us. A pass. The second couldn't contain a smile. A pass. The third's gaze went down to the floor and stayed there. A failed. The fourth was the sergeant. He stood a little more erect than usual and stared into the middle distance. A fail.

So far, a 50 per cent failure rate.

The fifth threw back his shoulders and beamed. A pass. The sixth man's head bowed, chin on chest. A fail. I later saw that he was crying. The marine was the seventh, and when he looked at his slip he gave a hollow laugh. He had been recommended to try again.

Then it was my turn. My heart was beating like a drum. Blood roared in my ears.

As the captain reached me I saw my paper. It had the second and third lines crossed out. The joy and relief were indescribable. All that I had been through had ultimately proved worthwhile.

Out of our group of ten, six of us were recommended to go forward to OCTU.

I was to report to Eaton Hall on Sunday, 17th August, 1952 for the four-month course. As this was three weeks away I was sent home on a fortnight's leave.

It was a very enjoyable leave. My father had bought me a motorbike. I was enjoying the company of my girlfriend, Kath, in every way. And it was summer.

The day I was given my motorbike, a Francis Barnet, I took a long drive over the Derbyshire hills. Well into the open countryside, miles from anywhere, it broke down. I checked the petrol was going through and that the plug was sparking properly. Completely foxed as to what was wrong, I lay on the grass to consider the situation.

Suddenly, out of nowhere, six motorcyclists roared past. About a hundred yards along the road they swerved like a swarm of bees and came thundering back. 'Having trouble?' one of them asked. They dismounted, took out an efficient looking tool-kit and set to work. In no time my pride and joy was in pieces on the grass verge. I looked on helplessly, wondering whether they could ever put it back together again.

But in no time at all they had. Then they leapt on to their bikes and shot off without a word. I tentatively mounted and lightly nudged the kick-starter. The engine smoothly sprang into life. I was extremely grateful to those taciturn but highly knowledgeable knights of the road.

I had to report to the depot at Wrexham three days before moving on to Eaton Hall. And I was mindful that having passed my WOSBY did not mean it was all plain sailing from then on. Far from it. Apart from the fact that officer cadet training was in itself very tough, there was the permanent threat of being 'returned to unit'. To be RTU'd was like being sent down from a university. If you were thrown out of OCTU there was no chance of returning and you did not receive your commission.

The journey from Wrexham to Eaton Hall took only twenty minutes and I rode there on my motorcycle. Eaton Hall, a red brick Victorian edifice, looked for all the world like St Pancras Station dropped into the middle of rural Cheshire. Understandably, as both were built by the same architect, Sir George Gilbert Scott. The present Duke of Westminster, whom I have had the pleasure of meeting on a number of occasions, has since replaced it with a modern building, leaving only the old stables standing.

It was pleasantly quiet as I rode up to some huts in front of the main building. I saw an area of tarmac beyond them and accelerated towards it. Suddenly I was in a vast open space and realised, to my absolute horror, that I had driven on to the parade square. The ultimate sacrilege!

Worse, before I could stop myself, I drove between a sergeant major and the squad he was drilling! Clutched by panic, I roared off the square, the sergeant major's stream of abuse ringing in my ears.

You've done it this time, Roache, I thought. You'll be RTU'd on your first day!

There was no question of me not being identified so it was just a matter of time before the inevitable explosion. I parked my bike and went in through the entrance to the main building. I was told where my room was and given a map of the camp. I was also instructed to take my battledress uniforms to the camp tailor to have officer cadets' white collar tabs sewn on. I was wondering if it was worth the effort.

As I was unpacking, an immaculate figure strode into my room. The Regimental Sergeant Major, the sergeant majors and most of the sergeants at Eaton Hall were from the Brigade of Guards, a very different breed of men to the ones I was used to. They all looked as though they had metal rods in place of spines. The peaks of their hats were flattened over their eyes and on to their nose, forcing the head back on to the neck in order to see anything. Their uniforms were impeccable and their physical presence awesome.

My visitor answered this description to a tee.

I had mistakenly thought it had been a sergeant major on the square, but I now discovered it was a sergeant from the Coldstream Guards. And he was standing in front of me.

'Officer Cadet Roache?'

'Yes, Sergeant,' I confessed, feeling like a man awaiting execution.

'You had the audacity to drive your infernal machine across the square while I was on it, didn't you, sir?'

'Yes, Sergeant.'

'Be at the company office at 0925 tomorrow morning for company orders.'

At the door he turned and added, 'Bloody good start to your training isn't it, sir?'

I had never before heard the word 'sir' used so effectively as a term of abuse.

As I continued unpacking I was convinced that in the morning I would be re-packing and returning to my unit.

The morning parade was an amazing example of military efficiency. Afterwards, everyone was dismissed except for us, the new platoon, in order that the RSM could honour us with a few words.

'Welcome to Eaton Hall, gentlemen. If you enjoy your stay with us it will mean either you're a masochist or we've failed in our duty. While you are here all NCOs will address you as sir. I will address you as sir, and you will address me as sir. The only difference being that you will mean it! You, sir, what is your name?'

'Cuthbert, sir.'

'Look at your boots, sir! They are an idle pair of boots! Take them for a run around the obelisk!'

A run round the obelisk, which stood at the top of the drive leading to Eaton Hall, was about a half-mile trip. It was a regular punishment. There was hardly a parade when a cadet wasn't sent around the obelisk. On one occasion the whole platoon was sent round.

After parade our thirty-strong platoon was directed to a classroom. At 0915 the platoon commander entered. A platoon commander is usually a second lieutenant – we would all be platoon commanders upon being commissioned – but the platoon commander here was a captain, as he was in charge of our instruction. Captain Adams, of the Warwickshire Regiment, was a pleasant and gentle man.

He was just starting to explain the routine when I stood up and said, 'Excuse me, sir.' He was surprised at so early an interruption.

'Yes?'

'May I be dismissed, sir? I'm on company orders in five minutes,' I said, feeling like I was digging my own grave with every word.

'Oh, well, in that case you'd better go.'

I left the classroom thinking what a brilliant introduction to my platoon commander this had been. A really good start to my training. If there was to be any training.

At the company office I found the offended sergeant waiting, rigid and immaculate as always, along with the Company Sergeant Major. 'Right, officer cadet, stand by that door,' the CSM said. He then went through the door and after a brief exchange of words came out and shouted, 'Officer Cadet Roache atteeeeenshun.! Riiiiight turn! Quiiiiick march! Left, right, left, right, left, right! Left turn, right turn! Halt! Salute!'

I was now facing a table behind which sat a major, with a dog by his side. 'Officer Cadet Roache, sir!' the CSM announced. 'He is charged with driving a motorbike across the square while the duty sergeant was inspecting the guard, sir! The sergeant who was on duty is here to give evidence when you are ready, sir!'

'Okay, wheel him in, Sergeant Major,' the major said.

There was a lot of stamping and saluting until the sergeant was in place at the table beside me.

'Right, Sergeant, tell me what happened.'

'Yes, sir!' the sergeant shouted. In fact, he bellowed all of his evidence. 'At approximately 1530 hours yesterday I was inspecting the new guard on the square! Suddenly there was this horrible noise and a motorcycle and rider appeared from nowhere and drove between me and the guard squad! I shouted for him to halt but he left at great speed! Never in all my time in the army have I witnessed anything like this, sir! It showed disrespect for me, the Army and all that I believe in, sir! I felt humiliated, sir! My authority was undermined, sir!'

I had the distinct impression the major did not really like all this noise. He dismissed the sergeant, who looked a little frustrated, and turned his attention to me.

'Well, Roache, what the devil were you doing?' He said this mildly, and my hopes rose as I saw a slight twinkle in his eye.

'I'm terribly sorry, sir,' I began. 'I'd just arrived and was a bit lost amongst the huts and drove on to what I thought was a parking area. I really did not mean to upset the sergeant, sir.'

The major leant back in his chair. 'Well, Roache, I think the sergeant *was* a little upset, don't you?'

'Yes, sir.'

'You won't do it again, will you, Roache?'

'*No*, sir!' A sense of optimism started welling up in me.

'All right, you'd better stay in camp for a week. Now off you go, there's a good chap.'

I could have hugged him. It was apparent that the major and the sergeant major enjoyed what had happened to the offended sergeant for some reason, and were amused by the whole incident.

I rejoined the class a very happy officer cadet. When we broke up, Captain Adams enquired about my company orders. As I told him, I noticed a half smile playing over his lips. I began to realise that far from harming my chances I had, if anything, enhanced them.

The work at Eaton Hall was hard, and if you fell behind you were jumped on severely, but everyone appreciated the necessity for this and gave their all. At the end of this training we would be second lieutenants and had to be ready to take up regimental duties and the command of a platoon. A platoon, incidently, consisted of one officer, a sergeant, three corporals and in all about forty men.

We were taught about the structure of the Army and its hierarchy, military tactics, military history, military law, man management, discipline, morale, domestic issues, teaching, training and motor transport. We were trained in the use of a range of weaponry, from the .38 revolver through the .303 rifle, sten gun, bren gun, 2″ and 3″ mortars and machinegun to the anti-tank gun. It was an awful lot to absorb in such a short period of time, but we were expected to be well-informed on all these subjects.

When we went out of camp in civilian clothes it was compulsory to wear a hat, because raising the hat is the only way to return a soldier's salute when in civvies. This created a bit of a problem for me as I was not a hat person. However, a difficult hour in a hat shop in Chester provided me with a dark-brown trilby and two ratting caps. The trilby, once rolled up at the sides and pulled down at the front, actually looked quite dashing and became a favourite part of my wardrobe.

A few weeks later I was part of a birthday celebration which took the form of a Saturday night pub-crawl. Food was forgotten as we careered erratically in a cadet's car from pub to pub. At about 10.00 p.m. we were weaving down a country lane when I had to ask the driver to pull over as I was not feeling too good. The car skidded to a halt. I opened the back door, stuck my head out and the trilby fell off. I was sick into it. The timing would have done credit to a comedy sketch.

*   *   *

In what seemed like no time we were participating in the passing-out parade that marked the end of our training. This was performed in front of our parents and the general public, as well as a very distinguished group of high-ranking military personnel.

That parade took place at midday on Friday, 5th December, 1952, the same day we were commissioned. I was now Second Lieutenant W.P. Roache, a fully commissioned officer in the British Army.

For some, the outcome of their time at Eaton Hall was less happy. There was one suicide while I was there, and I heard of two others in the preceding months. The one that happened during my stay was of a cadet who was offered his commission but not in the Guards regiment of his choice. Apparently it was of great family importance.

We were now due our Christmas leave. But before we left we had to go to the main hall to find out where and when to report for our postings afterwards. There was a large chart on the wall which gave this information, and I joined the throng of newly-fledged young officers clustered around it. It was some time before I found my name. When I did, I couldn't believe what I saw.

I can see those words in my mind now: SECOND LIEUTENANT W.P. ROACHE. POSTING. 1ST BATTALION, ROYAL WELCH FUSILIERS. CARIBBEAN. I stared at it blankly, uncomprehending. I was not even sure what the Caribbean meant, and as far as I knew all the RWF battalions were in Korea.

But gradually the truth dawned and a wonderful warm glow filled me. Life had never seemed so good. The dark clouds on the horizon rolled away and there was nothing but sunshine and joy. I had a very strong feeling that someone, or something, was looking after me. It was truly blissful.

I had a very enjoyable Christmas, not suspecting it would be my last in Rutland House.

Four

On 7th January, 1953 I was given a travel warrant to get myself and my luggage to Stansted airport for the flight to Kingston, Jamaica.

At Stansted I was directed to an area run by the RAF, and in a Nissen hut met my ten travelling companions. A captain in the Pay Corps, Captain Castle, was in command of the party, which consisted of six NCOs and other ranks, and two wives, one with a small child.

I was trying not to let it show, but I was feeling very nervous as this was the first time I had ever flown, and didn't really know what to expect. Eventually an RAF sergeant appeared and asked us to follow him. It felt very cold as we walked over the open tarmac, and my blood ran even colder when I realised we were heading for the only plane in sight – an ancient, camouflaged Hudson bomber. I knew it was a Hudson because I'd made a model of one at school. It was powered by two propeller-driven engines, and the thought of having to rely on those to get us across the Atlantic was not a happy one.

We entered by means of a short ladder through a hole in the side. The seats were canvas stretched over a tubular steel frame, and our luggage was in full view strapped down behind us. It was all very basic.

Some mechanics were fuelling the plane and managed to

crash a large piece of apparatus into one of the propellers. After a brief discussion, one of the mechanics produced a hammer and hit the end of the propeller with it. The pilot then climbed into the plane and started that engine. After a while he turned it off and climbed out again.

The pilot and ground crew gathered round the propeller once more. One of the mechanics touched it and hastily withdrew his hand. It was obviously very hot. The hammer was again produced and further blows directed at the propeller. After this they all seemed happy. The pilot and his crew of two climbed aboard and the hole in the side was filled with an oval piece of fuselage they called a door.

This was all a bit worrying.

We were then told that as the Hudson was incapable of flying directly to Jamaica we were going via Iceland and Nova Scotia. The geography of this seemed a little strange to me. But I was in their hands and thought the best thing to do was to pretend it wasn't happening.

The pilot started the engines. We lurched down the runaway and – miraculously – into the air.

It wasn't easy to talk, with the noise and vibration, and there was nothing to see. Had it not been for my ability to sleep at any time and in almost any place, the journey would have been extremely unpleasant as well as frightening.

But the best was yet to come.

We landed at Reykjavik in Iceland and were accommodated at the American airbase, which was very pleasant and comfortable. This was just as well because, unsurprisingly, there turned out to be a mechanical fault with the Hudson. This needed spare parts to be flown out and we were there for five days while it was repaired.

On the fifth day we were told the Hudson was now ready and we would take off at noon. After about two hours of cold, uncomfortable flight we noticed the plane was shuddering more than usual. The sky was pitch black and I was all too aware that only the freezing Atlantic lay below us. I must admit I was terrified. Then the pilot handed over to his co-pilot and came to talk to us. Shouting over the racket he told us we were just off the foot of Greenland, and over half-way on our journey, but that the headwinds were so strong we were hardly moving. We were going to have to turn back to Reykjavik. A further two days were passed there waiting for the weather to improve.

Eventually we got to Halifax, Nova Scotia. I received the news that the Hudson had suffered a further mechanical failure and it would be a few days before we could continue our journey with numbed resignation. Another six days passed.

It was thirteen days after taking off from Stansted that we embarked on the final leg of our journey to Kingston.

The first thing that hit me as I stepped on to Jamaican soil was the heat. It was like a furnace after Iceland and Nova Scotia. The second was the smell, a not unpleasant mixture of spices and fish, which remains linked to my memories of Kingston to this day.

A small group of military vehicles was lined up by the side of the runway. Standing nearby were two second lieutenants, a duty sergeant and four men, all very brown, in their tropical uniforms. We must have seemed very white and overdressed to them.

One of the second lieutenants introduced himself as Philip Knight and asked me to get my men organised. I did not feel the slightest bit inclined to get anyone organised, but fortunately the sergeant came forward and generally sorted everyone out. Captain Castle was taken off in a separate vehicle and I was to see him only once, very briefly, over the next twelve months.

The other second lieutenant sauntered over, shook hands and introduced himself as Selwyn Hughes, saying he had just come along for the ride. He was particularly pleased to see me, as up to then he had been the junior subaltern and now I would have the honour of filling that post.

I immediately warmed to Selwyn and we became good,

indeed lifelong, friends. He still writes to me occasionally from his home in Australia. In fact it was living out there that made him eligible to appear on my *This is Your Life*, as it is *de rigueur* to produce someone from the antipodes on these occasions.

Our sleeping quarters at Up Park Camp, like most of the other buildings, was made of wood and sat on raised posts. And all the rooms had their own verandah. Mine, which had a bare wooden floor, contained the usual wardrobe, table and chairs, a large fan in the ceiling and a mosquito net over the bed. In a few weeks' time I would wake up in the night and look with horror at this mosquito net as just above my face something dark, about the size of a tennis ball, was slowly crawling up it. Drenched in sweat, I slowly put a hand out of the net and switched on the light. Tarantulas were quite common in Jamaica, but this was the mess kitten.

Selwyn took me to the mess, where we had banana sandwiches, and fresh orange juice with sugar served in large silver goblets. This proved a daily tea-time delight. Rum was tuppence a tot. When it was made into a long drink with fresh lime and sugar you did not notice the rum. This delightfully deceptive concoction was the cause of many a boozy night and terrible hangover. Other favourite tipples were Tom Collins and sometimes the local beer, Red Stripe, which has become something of a cult drink in Britain in the last few years.

The following morning I reported to my commanding officer, Lieutenant Colonel Johnson, the highest ranking officer, other than the board of WOSBY, I had so far come into contact with. I was totally unprepared for what I saw. Colonel Johnson was a broad, fair-haired, pleasant looking man wearing a patterned, brightly coloured, short-sleeve shirt, bermuda shorts and sandals. Having so far in my Army career been accustomed to strict formality in dress, this was a little surprising.

'Come in, Mr Roache,' he said warmly. 'Shut the door and sit down. Did you have a good journey?'

He went on to tell me the battalion was under strength, that he expected his officers to play polo, and that his main concern was a forthcoming four-day tattoo to celebrate the Queen's coronation.

'You are going to be in B company, commanded by Major Tolhurst,' he continued. 'Unfortunately, we are so far under strength you will not have a platoon, but you will have a sergeant. And I have a job for you.'

Shortly, he explained, a ship was due from the UK. On board would be £4,000 worth of fireworks – an enormous amount of money in 1953 – and my task was to divide them into four displays, one for each day of the tattoo. I was also to be in charge of the actual displays.

I was still absorbing this when he added, 'Oh, by the way, do you play bridge?'

'Yes, Colonel.'

'Good, you can make up a four when I'm short.'

It was a bit of a comedown from platoon commander to running firework displays. But I consoled myself with the thought that at least it was a branch of showbiz.

As I made my way across the hot, dusty square to B company's lines, a voice boomed out, 'I'm saluting you, sir!' It was the Regimental Sergeant Major and I quickly returned his salute.

RSM Turvey, I soon learnt, was in the habit of approaching any officer whose appearance did not meet with his approval and saying, 'I shall have to have a word with your batman, sir. If I see you dressed like that again, sir, I will put him on a charge.' Like the RSM at Eaton Hall, he had the knack of making 'sir' sound like a term of abuse, only his approach was a little more subtle. RSM Turvey was in fact a splendid soldier, and I grew to like and respect him.

There seemed to be no one about as I approached B company's office. Then a company sergeant major shot out of the door. He stamped to attention, saluted and shouted, 'Company Sergeant Major Slater, sir! Welcome to B company!'

Then an officer sauntered out of another door, hands in the pockets of his khaki shorts, service hat on the side of his head and a pipe in his mouth. He was accompanied by a dog which looked for all the world like a sawn-off crocodile.

'You're Mr Roache I presume, sir,' CSM Slater ventured. 'This is Major Tolhurst, the company commander.'

'Shut up, Oscar,' the Major said, turning back into his office and presumably intending me to follow.

Inside, seated on hard, straight-backed chairs, Major Tolhurst's attitude was equally casual. 'We haven't got a platoon for you, you know. We can only scrape one together out of the whole company and that bugger Selwyn has got it.'

'Yes, sir, I under – '

'For God's sake call me Guy,' he said gruffly. 'So I don't really know what to do with you.'

'That's all right, sir . . . er . . . Guy.' At that stage I found it very difficult to call anyone in authority by their first name. 'The CO has given me a job looking after the fireworks for the coronation tattoo.'

'Well, good luck to you then. He's like a bloody old woman with those fireworks. Do you play cricket?'

'Yes, si . . . er . . . yes, I do.'

I little realised the particular door those words were to open.

Cricket was a major preoccupation at the camp. We played most weekends and sometimes during the week. Guy Tolhurst demonstrated a superb ability at the game, and ran the battalion team very successfully. This was remarkable because it seemed to me that most Jamaicans could play cricket before they could walk. Where there was a group of barefoot children, you would like as not find a cricket bat and ball.

Sometimes we travelled to a plantation that had its own cricket field, and as the day wore on, drinks – and I mean *drinks* – would be brought on to the field. There were always people playing guitars or steel bands around, and you never quite knew when the game ended and the party began. The hardest part of life during this period was coping with the hangovers.

Guy Tolhurst and Company Sergeant Major Slater were at opposite ends of the spectrum. CSM Slater, the classic ramrod military type who lived by the book, was later to become a sergeant major at Sandhurst. Guy Tolhurst, on the other hand, knew he would not advance beyond the rank of major and was due to retire in a few years. He was only in the Army because he didn't know what else to do after the war, and just wanted to see out his time with minimum effort and responsibility.

He wasn't bitter, and he wasn't a rebel in the sense that he would cause trouble. He was simply not interested in being a good soldier. He drank a lot, although I never saw him drunk; he would bite your head off and was often rude and uncommunicative. He could be really nasty if he didn't like you. Selwyn and I nicknamed him Beasthurst.

But underneath he was a big softie and, in my opinion, a non-practising homosexual. I say non-practising because, although in the eighteen months I worked closely with him he never made any sort of advance towards me nor, to my knowledge, anyone else, although I knew I was a favourite.

I was aware of very little homosexuality in the Army which, considering it was almost entirely a male ghetto in those days, is perhaps surprising. I came across it only once in my five years' service, and this was while I was in Jamaica. I was duty officer when a military police sergeant asked if I and the guard commander would accompany him in an attempt to catch one of the storemen in a homosexual act.

Six of us, equipped with torches, accompanied the military police sergeant on a night-time raid on the battalion store. He asked us to be very quiet and positioned us in a semi-circle at the back of the store, where there were quite a few windows and some double doors that were half glass. He placed himself by one of these doors and said the minute he switched on his torch we were to do the same.

I was standing there in the dark reflecting on the fact that I found this particular task rather distasteful, when suddenly the MP sergeant's torch flashed into life. As instructed, we directed ours through the windows, too. The blaze of light picked up a mattress on the floor. On it was the storeman and a young fusilier, both naked from the waist down. I assume there was a surprised look on their faces but from my viewpoint it was impossible to tell as all I could see were two bare bottoms. The MP sergeant went in and arrested them.

Apparently the military police had been after the storeman for some time, suspecting he had been using his position to swop material favours for sexual ones. Fortunately, I was not needed at the court martial, where the storeman was dismissed from the service. The young fusilier was treated quite leniently on the plea that he had been heavily influenced by the older man.

Misbehaviour of a quite different kind also curtailed the career of Philip Knight, who had been orderly officer on the day of my arrival.

Philip had some strange ideas, one of which was that we should all call other ranks by their christian names. Friendly though this might be, it was against Army regulations and probably bad for discipline, and I wondered why, if he felt so strongly about it, he had agreed to take his commission.

He was discovered stealing some money from a fellow officer and placed under room-arrest, where we took it in turns to sit with him. He was court martialled, found guilty, and dismissed from the service. I felt this was a bit severe, but as he was coming to the end of his National Service anyway, it was perhaps the best solution.

*　　*　　*

In due course, word of the fireworks' arrival reached us. As the CO and I were driven to the docks he talked excitedly about what type of fireworks there were, how he had personally selected them and what a splendid display it was going to be. I felt a little like a father taking his excited offspring for a half-term treat. But I had grown fond of Colonel Johnson and felt very much at ease with him.

On arrival at the docks, we drove straight into a large warehouse, at the far end of which about twenty large crates were being loaded on to lorries by a party of fusiliers. The colonel leapt out of the car and strode over. He pointed to a particular crate and ordered a rather startled fusilier to open it. With gleeful triumph the colonel held aloft a five-foot rocket with a head of about eighteen inches. 'Magnificent,' he said, 'magnificent.'

The fireworks were taken to a big dry storeroom near to the battalion carpenter, from where we set about arranging the displays and building the necessary apparatus for firing them. The first thing we built were sloping ramps from which to launch the rockets; then tall posts supported by ropes were erected, rather like washing lines, to hold the long strand of the fireworks called 'Niagara Falls'.

The hardest problem was supporting the massively heavy sixteen-foot, firework encrusted, portraits of the Queen which were to provide the centre point of the displays. We ended up building thirty-foot bamboo towers to mount them on. I remember climbing one and getting a touch of vertigo as it swayed precariously from side to side. There were only two of these portraits and the first and last days of the tattoo were considered the best times to use them.

My appointed assistant, Sergeant Duffissey, had little to do at this stage and spent most of his time in the sergeants' mess enjoying bottles of Red Stripe. On the actual days of the tattoo, however, his role would be crucial, as he and I would be lighting the fireworks in a carefully planned sequence.

The big day was rapidly upon us. The ramps, the tower

and all the fireworks for the first night were in place. I had carefully explained and rehearsed the sequence of firing with Sergeant Duffissey, and told him to meet me on site half an hour before we were due to start.

With just twenty minutes to go there was no sign of him. I sent an urgent message to the sergeants' mess and, with less than five minutes left, the sergeant lurched out of the darkness towards me.

'Where the hell have you been?' I snapped.

'Shorry, shurr,' he said, gently swaying.

The Red Stripe had taken its toll. He was smashed out of his mind. I was worried about leaving him in charge of the rockets, but with one minute to go there was no choice.

'Can you remember what to do?'

'Yesssir.'

'Okay. Light the wick and stand by the first batch. When I drop my arm you ignite them. Have you got that?'

'Yesssir.'

I ran over to position myself by the first of the major fireworks. Looking back, I saw Sergeant Duffissey fumbling with the matches in an attempt to light the wick. Then I saw the flash and red smoulder as he managed it.

I dropped my arm to signal the start. The smouldering red tip weaved about. With relief I saw the glow of the touch paper on the first rocket. Sergeant Duffissey then lurched toward the second one. What seemed an age passed as he tried to light it. By now at least six rockets should have been lit.

Suddenly a spray of sparks spurted out of the first rocket. Simultaneously, Sergeant Duffisey staggered backwards, knocking it sideways. The spray of sparks and fire shot down the whole length of the ramp, igniting in one go all the rockets for the entire display. Seeing this I dashed around and lit every one of my fireworks as quickly as possible in order to preserve some kind of sequence.

The display, intended to last ten minutes, was over in two.

Having established that Sergeant Duffissey, apart from being drunk, was in good health, I slumped despondently on the grass in my scorched shirt. Then the colonel came running over to me. Oh, God, I thought, now I'm for it. And stood up to face the tirade.

'Well done, Mr Roache!' he exclaimed. 'Smashing. Haven't enjoyed myself so much for ages. Keep it up!'

So it was that a ten-minute display became a two-minute display for the remaining three days.

A few more fusiliers were shipped in and we managed to make up two half-strength platoons, one commanded by Selwyn and the other by me. With the help of the sergeant I worked out a training schedule and set about turning my platoon into a mean fighting force. Well, that was the intention. But with regular demands for working parties, battalion parades and duties, guard duties, cleaning company lines, a disinterested company commander, cricket, the heat and hangovers to deal with, it wasn't an easy task.

My friendship with Selwyn was now well-established and I really enjoyed his company. He was a great talker and I was not, so we made a good pair. Having been commissioned just before me he was of course my senior. This meant that whenever Major Tolhurst was absent, which was not infrequently, Selwyn would have to take the company parade and I would have to march up to him and report the company present. He would also deal with disciplinary matters. Selwyn would sometimes tease me about this and I must confess to finding it a little irksome. Much later, when our promotions came through to full lieutenant, half the time we had spent in the ranks was added towards seniority and this moved me ahead of Selwyn. So now the tables were turned and I took the parades and company orders. Much to his chagrin.

Selwyn wrote poetry, which was pretty good but, I thought, just a hobby. But he was later to become a successful poet and novelist. As I write, he has just sent me from Australia a poem for my sixtieth birthday, recalling, among other things, my flight landing in Jamaica and our first meeting.

Selwyn and I disagree about politics and religious matters, we meet rarely and correspond infrequently, but I regard him as one of my closest friends. I have recently had the pleasure of escorting him for two days when he was over here promoting his book of poems, *Stirring Stuff*.

A suggestion from a colonel is tantamount to an order, and before too long I was reminded that Colonel Johnson expected his officers to play polo. Consequently I reported to the stables for instruction.

I'd done a certain amount of riding, so this was of no great concern to me, but I was worried about the cost. We had to pay a monthly mess bill, mainly for drinks, but it included other items bought through the officers' mess. If I took up polo, apart from having to acquire all the gear, I would be responsible for the keep of the horses. This would be an enormous drain on an already much depleted salary.

The sergeant in charge of the stables was waiting for me with a horse all tacked up. He started with some preliminary chat about the game and demonstrated how the stick should be held. He handed the stick over to me and I gripped it with my left hand.

'No, no, sir. It must be held in the *right* hand,' he said firmly.

'I am sorry, Sergeant,' I told him, 'but I'm totally left-handed. I'm quite useless with my right hand.'

'In that case, sir, I have some bad news for you,' he stated gravely. I suspected it wasn't going to be at all bad as far as I was concerned.

'Apart from being dangerous and having difficulties with the horse,' he explained, 'you will fall foul of the offside rule. I'm afraid that you will not be permitted to play with your left hand, sir.'

'Oh dear, sergeant,' I said, trying to look genuinely disappointed, 'and I was so looking forward to it. Is there nothing I can do?'

'It's impossible, sir. Wouldn't be allowed.'

My left-handedness had released me, with honour, from the colonel's 'suggestion'.

Any fusiliers and other ranks going out for a night on the town in Kingston had first to report to the guardroom, which was also the PAC – the Prophylactic Aid Centre. There the outgoing soldier would be issued with a condom, and on his return had to state if he had had sexual intercourse and how much time had elapsed since the incident. This information was entered in a special book. He would then have to wash his private parts with a disinfectant. If a soldier failed to do this and caught VD it was regarded as a self-inflicted wound and he could be placed on a charge.

This may all seem Draconian, not to say overly bureaucratic, but the temptations in Kingston were legion. Every night the road leading to the camp gates was lined with a dozen or more Jamaican women selling themselves, and it was difficult to approach or leave the camp on foot without being solicited. I remember one girl shouting at me, 'You like a nice clean girl? All pink inside like Queen Victoria?'

I remember the Medical Officer telling me he reckoned that during the RWF tour of duty in Jamaica about 70 per cent of the battalion contracted some form of venereal disease.

In the MO's office there was a row of blood samples waiting to be tested for VD, with the name, rank and number of the soldiers concerned written on the bottles. There were also a few marked 'X1', 'X2', etc. These were the officers' samples.

Some of the brothels in Kingston were out of bounds for one reason or another and the military police made surprise raids on them from time to time. The duty officer was often asked to go along on these raids, but during my twelve months in Jamaica this task fell to me only once.

The party consisted of a sergeant major, four military policemen and myself. We were visiting just one brothel to check there were no RWF personnel enjoying its hospitality.

Our truck pulled up in front of a large wooden house with a verandah. In no time we were through the front door and into a reception and bar area. The sergeant major detailed two MPs to check everyone there and the rest of us dashed upstairs to the 'working' area. We opened the door to a bedroom and found a young fusilier, wearing only a short unbuttoned tropical shirt and socks, being entertained by a naked black girl.

The young man shot off the bed, stood rigidly to attention and ejaculated. I doubt he was brought to orgasm by the sight of us and put it down to a very unusual example of *coitus interruptus*. The sergeant major said, 'Now you've finished coming, fusilier, you can get going. You're under arrest!'

Back in the corridor, several other doors were open, with girls standing in them trying to entice us in and treating the whole thing as a big joke. Then a shout from one of the MPs had us all crowding into a small bathroom to find the bottom half of another fusilier stuck in a small window through which he had been attempting to escape. He was quite firmly jammed, and releasing him caused severe grazing which subsequently needed treatment. Not that this prevented him being arrested.

I don't know what happened to the two fusiliers as they were not in B company, but the usual punishment was two weeks confined to barracks.

The Royal Welch, of course, celebrated St David's Day with style. There was a full battalion parade, complete with band and regimental goat. In the evening there was a mess night at which the Governor of Jamaica, Sir Hugh Foot – the brother of Dingle and Michael Foot – was the guest of honour.

Normally our batmen would have woken us but, having prepared our uniforms, they had themselves to get ready for the big parade. So it was agreed that Selwyn would wake me by banging on the wall when his alarm went off at 7.00 am. This would give us time to get into our starched uniforms, have a quick standing-up coffee in the mess and be on parade by 0815.

I was roused by a frantic banging on the wall and Selwyn yelling, 'Bill, Bill, I overslept! It's 7.30!'

'Bloody hell, Selwyn!' I exclaimed, leaping out of bed.

I got washed, shaved and dressed in record-breaking time. Fifteen minutes later I was ready and just putting my sword in place when there was another knock on the wall and Selwyn shouted, 'Bill, I'm sorry. I got it wrong. It's only 6.30.'

There I was, feeling tired, harassed, starched and unable to sit down with nearly two hours still to go before the parade. There were lots of things I wanted to say. I settled for, 'You're a bit of a twerp, aren't you, Selwyn?'

It was the first of a string of disasters that day.

The battalion was being formed up in companies by the RSM as we arrived at the parade ground. A company was away in Belize so B company was at the front. This meant Guy Tolhurst would be the leading officer, with Selwyn and myself just behind him. As we marched to our places, Selwyn said out of the side of his mouth, 'When we fall in, do we stay at attention or stand at ease?'

'I don't know.'

'Whatever Guy does,' Selwyn suggested, 'we had better do the opposite.'

We fell in with the whole battalion behind us and just Guy in front, who remained at attention. So Selwyn and myself stood at ease. There was a short pause then the second in command, Major Bosanquet, was heard to say to his adjutant, 'Why are Mr Roache and Mr Hughes standing at ease when the battalion is standing to attention?'

The adjutant came forward and shouted, 'Mr Roache and Mr Hughes, ATTEEEEEN-SHUN!' Up to now every order had been followed by the vibrating thud of a thousand feet stamping in unison. Now there was the feeble clomp of just two.

The battalion then marched to the sports ground where we were stood at ease and a long wait began. And it was a particularly hot day.

Over the peak of my service hat came an ant. Followed by another. Then another. My hands were held behind my back in the at-ease position and we were not allowed to move. In an attempt to get rid of them I stuck out my bottom lip and blew upwards as the ants crawled down my face.

It didn't work.

The ants crawled further down my face and on to my neck. I was sweating enough with the heat and could have done without this. Eventually they went on to my uniform. Thank God they didn't go *under* it. Apart from the thought of them, they were no further trouble.

I was just breathing a discreet sigh of relief when I heard a gentle moan and a thud behind me. Sneaking a look, I saw that a fusilier had fainted. Glancing across to the other companies I could see gaps in the ranks, like missing teeth, marking the absence of a fainted fusilier. Nobody was allowed to move. Those who fainted lay there.

The sergeant behind me addressed the platoon in a loud whisper: 'Raise yourselves gently on the balls of your feet, without being noticed. Can you hear me? Raise yourselves on the balls of your feet!' This tensed the muscles in the legs and squeezed out the blood, helping it to circulate better. But more than that it provided something to think about rather than fainting fusiliers. Until the bandsman with the big drum went down with a loud boom, and the goat major fainted, leaving the goat to wander off.

The relief all of us felt when that particular inspection came to an end was tremendous.

Five

Later on, the Colonel called an officers meeting to tell us we were going to be part of the security arrangements for the 'big three' conference in Bermuda. The 'big three' were Churchill, Eisenhower and the French president, who bore the rather unfortunate name Bidet. The talks were held at the Mid Ocean golf club, probably on Eisenhower's recommendation.

The Bermudians were delighted at our presence and we were in great demand socially. A very wealthy diamond dealer, with eighteen-year-old twin daughters, invited Selwyn and myself to dinner. When the meal was over, our host said, 'Now we have a special treat for you, which my wife has gone to great lengths to prepare correctly.'

This lady then walked in with two plates. 'There you are,' she said proudly, 'Yorkshire pudding.' And they all sat back and looked at us. I broke out in a sweat. I had a small appetite in those days, was already full, and had never been able to eat Yorkshire pudding anyway. But we had no choice other than to set about it. A task *well* above and beyond the call of duty.

All the twins wanted to know about were hunt balls, and we could have developed a very good relationship with them if Selwyn had not gone over the top and told them he was the Right Honourable Selwyn. And that I was Lord Roache of Nottingham. To save ourselves further embarrassment we had to avoid them for the rest of our stay.

On our return to Jamaica I was transferred to Support Company and put in command of a three-inch mortar platoon. This meant that instead of marching everywhere, we travelled in trucks or land rovers, which was much more civilised.

Almost immediately, word arrived that there was trouble brewing in British Guyana. An insurrection was feared and the governor had requested the Royal Welch Fusiliers should come and save the day. Our battalion was in no fit state to save anybody's day. Nevertheless our arrival in Georgetown apparently did the trick of frightening off the revolutionaries, although our duties consisted of little more than marching around, breaking up groups of more than three people.

The only blood spilt was when a major unloading his revolver shot a subaltern in the leg. Fortunately it was a flesh wound.

Having heroically put down the rebellion, we had some free time on our hands, and I was persuaded to go on an alligator shoot. A sergeant, two fusiliers and myself set off in a wooden canoe paddled by two Guyanese guides. The trip was fascinating. For most of the time the incredibly verdant jungle came right up to the riverbank. The trees were filled with brightly coloured birds, and at one point we passed a small stretch of mud bank visible between the jungle's edge and the water. Sliding across this was the brown and green body of a snake about ten inches in diameter, its head submerged in the muddy water while its tail was still in the jungle.

'Anaconda,' said one of our guides. I'd heard that giant anacondas could be thirty feet in length, and didn't at all like the idea that one of these could be swimming along under our small boat.

After a couple of hours we came to another mud bank on which two alligators were basking. One immediately scuttled into the water. I fired my rifle and the other alligator rolled over and lay still. The canoe was pulled on to the bank and we cautiously approached the motionless creature. It was not big as alligators go, being about six feet in length, and we pulled it into the canoe, laying it flat along the bottom under the seats.

We decided this was as good a time as any to have our packed lunches and retired to a clearing nearby. When we returned to the canoe we found to our horror that the alligator was very much alive. And snapping.

Fortunately the narrowness of the canoe and the seats had it well-confined and made it impossible for it to escape or inflict any damage. On the other hand, it was too dangerous for us to get into the canoe. And we couldn't shoot the beast because a bullet would likely go through the bottom of the boat and we would be effectively stranded.

Eventually we hit on the idea of making a noose to go over the alligator's jaws. Getting it around the animal's gaping mouth was considerably easier said than done, but after a great deal of struggle we managed it. The jaws clamped shut, we then pulled its head over the side and shot it.

After a few weeks we left and returned to Kingston, and finally, in December, 1953, I was sent back to England. I was sent on ahead of my battalion so I could attend a three-inch mortar course due to begin on 11th January.

I left Jamaica with very fond memories of my colleagues, the people and the beautiful island itself. I counted myself extremely fortunate to have had a posting in such a wonderfully exotic place.

Christmas was celebrated on the banana boat which carried me home. There were seven or eight of us first-class passengers and, along with a much larger group of second-class passengers, most of whom were Jamaicans also going home, we all got together on Christmas day and sang carols. It was an absolutely wonderful, magical occasion.

*   *   *

I saw in the New Year with my family, then on 11th January reported to the Small Arms School for the planned three-inch mortar course.

We used live explosives for this training, and a frightening incident on one exercise left me with a legacy I bear to this day.

A mortar team consists of three men, and in the event of a problem or emergency there are a set of IAs – 'immediate actions' – they have to observe. A mortar round is propelled by an explosive charge which ignites when the bomb reaches the bottom of the barrel. On this occasion it failed to go off.

The IA in such circumstances is to slightly raise the barrel and gently shake it, because the most likely reason for a failure to fire is simply that the bomb has got stuck. But one of my companions was over-eager. He pulled the mortar totally upright, shook it violently and – *woomph* – off it went.

I was standing quite near the mouth of the mortar and the force of the detonation blasted my eardrum. I was virtually deaf for about three weeks and I've had a permanent hearing problem ever since. I can't hear a clock ticking, and on certain notes I'm almost stone deaf.

But the worst thing was that, as the angle of the mortar had been altered, this bomb went straight up in the air. And it was a high explosive charge.

We knew we had about thirty seconds before it came back to earth. But we had no idea where. The sergeant with us said, 'There's no point in running; you don't know how off it's going to be. Just get down everybody.' So we got down and waited for what seemed an eternity. Fortunately, it landed well away from us. That was one of the scariest, and longest, half-minutes of my life.

The man responsible was returned to his unit. He had put everyone's life at risk and was quite severely dealt with.

By the time I finished the course, my battalion was back

from Jamaica. But shortly after settling into camp at Swindon we received a posting to Dortmund in Germany.

We took part in a number of large-scale exercises there, carried out with allied armies, as part of the defence of Europe. It was really hard, strict regimental work, and I didn't greatly enjoy it. I realised how lucky I'd been to have had the posting to Jamaica. The relaxed, laid-back way of life there had been a lot of fun. The German posting was considerably less interesting and I was growing very bored and restless.

Then I heard that volunteers were sought for a peace-keeping force in the Persian Gulf. I knew little about what this entailed, except that officers were required to command Arab troops on behalf of Trucial Oman States. This had a romantic and dramatic air about it.

The first lesson you learn in the Army is never to volunteer for anything. But on this occasion I followed my gut instinct and put my name forward. I remember that when I went to the battalion adjutant about this he looked at me askance and commented, 'You must be mad.' Nevertheless, my application went forward.

To my astonishment, within two weeks I was sent home on embarkation leave. Obviously they were pretty desperate to fill the post. I still hadn't found out much about what would be required of me. Except for one significant fact – it wasn't a regimental job at all. I was to be seconded to the Foreign Office.

I went home and waited and waited. After a couple of months, during which nothing seemed to be happening, I took the initiative and rang the Ministry of Defence. 'Oh, good heavens!' they said. 'We'd forgotten all about you.' My travel papers promptly arrived and the wheels began turning at last.

Soon I was boarding the troopship *Dilwara* at Southampton, bound for Port Said. I was travelling with officers of the Leicestershire regiment, and they became increasingly curious about the nature of my mission. One of them said, 'Ah, it's cloak-and-dagger stuff, is it?' My lack of a response just confirmed their suspicions. But I didn't say anything because I didn't know what I was doing any more than they did.

From Port Said I was taken to a place called Faid in the canal zone. After about three weeks there I was flown to Bahrain. I now knew my ultimate destination was to be Sharjah, situated in the centre of the Oman States. The flight there was in a clapped-out Anson. They called the twin-engined Anson the cow of the air. It was a wonderful workhorse of a plane whose parts could be changed and replenished endlessly.

We were shortly flying over an endless terrain of desert. There was no sign of any kind of civilisation or habitation. After many hours, we approached a small collection of mud houses and what are called barusti, dwellings constructed from woven palm leaves. Nearby was a crude airstrip. The place was otherwise incredibly bleak and empty.

There was a small RAF contingent at Sharjah and one of their officers greeted me. HQ was located in a mud-brick fort, similar to the ones featured in the film versions of *Beau Geste*, and it was here that I met commanding officer Colonel Johnson. A coincidence this; there was no family relationship with the Colonel Johnson I served under in Jamaica.

'We've only got seven officers here,' he said, 'and you'll be taking over B squadron.' They were called squadrons because the command structure was based on tank regiments, presumably a hangover from the great desert battles of the Second World War. All squadron commanders had to be the rank of captain or above, and I had been temporarily promoted to this rank.

'Tragically,' Colonel Johnson added, 'the previous commander was shot by his own men.'

Now you tell me, I thought.

'You've got a week in which to learn some of the basic

language,' he went on, 'because you'll be in sole charge of a totally Arab contingent, most of them bedouins.'

So I spent the next seven days desperately learning the Arabic for words like 'water', 'food' and one or two other basics. Then I was shipped off to a remote outpost called Mirfa. Fortunately, there was one Arab officer there for a while who could speak English, but he stayed only for three or four weeks, leaving me in command of 140 arabs. These men were drawn from the seven sheikdoms of the Gulf, with the function of keeping peace between them; a kind of Middle Eastern UN force of its day.

Our area of responsibility had previously been known as the Pirate Coast. Added to this were the activities of one particular nomadic tribe, the Beni Kitab, who were very warlike. Their *modus operandi* was to arrive at one of the seven sheikdoms and send their men in to say, 'If you don't pay us in money or food we'll attack you.' They were brigands of a sort. But this had been going on for so many years it was almost regarded as an annual tax. Provided the Beni Kitab didn't ask for too much, or act too disruptively, people would pay them.

Later, when we took over, they were disarmed and told to behave themselves. Not unnaturally they were deeply upset about this. It had been their way of life for as long as anyone could remember and they saw no reason why they shouldn't carry on. But eventually they were brought into the fold as members of the seven sheikdoms' peace-keeping force.

So there I was in command of a squadron of troops drawn from a number of regions, all speaking local dialect variants of Arabic. I had one or two words of their language, they knew none in English. But surprisingly we rubbed along quite well, despite the obvious communication problems. It's amazing what you can do when you have to.

One thing I noticed was that if I gave an order to a sergeant he would sometimes walk over to a private soldier for a hushed consultation. Then the private would nod and the sergeant would carry out the order. I came to understand that in the tribal hierarchy some of the soldiers were very important, and although one of their fellows may have been promoted by us to sergeant, he was still lower in rank. You had to be a bit careful about things like that.

Our encampment was not far from the Buriemi Oasis, and this was where Sheik Sayed, who is now the Emir of the United Arab Emirates, was based. I got to know him quite well. He had a very basic sort of palace there and shortly after my arrival I was invited over to meet him.

This was in the days before these Arab states struck oil and became extremely wealthy, so, at this time, everything was very basic. Sheik Sayed owned a clapped-out American car and one or two aged Land Rovers. Food was brought in by camel.

I arrived to find him sitting on cushions at the far end of a long room with various tribal dignitaries ranged on either side. On this particular day he was holding court, and his people were lining up to pay their respects and ask certain favours of him. He beckoned me to sit down and I squatted nearby, fascinated by this age-old custom.

A supplicant would approach him with great deference, bow low and say, 'Salaam aleikum' – Peace be with you – the ancient Arab greeting. Then they made their request or asked for a judgment in some dispute or other. He would listen and then say either, '*la*', which means 'no' or 'naam', which is 'yes'. The man would thank him and go. There was no question of any quibbles.

I was incredibly impressed with the Sheik's dignity. His answers may have been monosyllabic, but you realised that what he said, he meant, and everyone treated him with very real respect.

We subsequently shared a meal together. And let me take this opportunity to scotch the idea that guests are offered sheep's eyeballs. They aren't regarded as the choicest bits.

I was in fact given sheep brains, the skull cracked open and its contents scooped out in front of me.

The food was served in one large dish placed on the floor between us. And one unbreakable tradition was that you ate with your right hand. The reason for using the right hand is that the left is the one used when going to the lavatory. Not that there were any lavatories, of course; the function was performed by finding a quiet place in the desert. Being totally left-handed, I had to take great care over this. If you reached for food with your left hand everyone regarded you with absolute horror. There may not have been much in the way of hygiene in other respects, but this was the one thing you didn't do.

Another social taboo was pointing your feet at anybody. That was regarded as extremely discourteous. I never really found out why, and could only suppose it was because the feet were invariably travel-worn and covered with sand. So you sat with your feet tucked underneath you.

But belching was certainly in order; indeed it was thought of as a sign that you enjoyed and approved of the fare set before you.

I had a photograph taken with Sheik Sayed at that time, for which I put on full Arab dress. I'm sorry to say I loaned it to a newspaper some years ago and it was never returned.

Not long after taking command of my squadron we heard that a hunting party from Qatar in the north, which was not in the seven sheikdom alliance, had crossed the border into Oman. My orders were to go and ask them to leave.

I set off with four or five Land Rovers full of soldiers and we eventually located the trespassers' camp. I thought it unwise to drive straight in with all the soldiers, so I approached in our Land Rover with just the sergeant major, two men and the driver. The rest of the soldiers stayed out of sight behind a sand dune nearby.

We were greeted quite respectfully, as is the desert custom.

In my halting Arabic, much of which had to be translated by the sergeant major, I asked them if they were aware of being in the territory of another sheikdom. They nodded and said yes. I formally requested that they move out. I don't know how my guide translated this but they just laughed, shrugged and stood their ground. They weren't being unpleasant, but they obviously had no intention of leaving.

Polite this exchange may have been, in a bizarre sort of way, but I was only too aware that this rather formidable looking bunch were bristling with rifles and daggers. Apart from the safety of my men and myself, I had to keep in mind that this was a delicate political situation. One wrong move and we had a potential international incident on our hands.

While I was pondering my next move, the Land Rovers containing the remainder of my group suddenly appeared. The sergeant I had left in charge of them, realising the delicacy of our position, had used his initiative and decided to back us up.

As soon as they saw this the attitude of the hunting party completely changed. The laughing and joking stopped and, without further discussion, they got into their vehicles and drove off. So a volatile situation had been defused without either side losing face. The all important dignity had been preserved.

I think the incident was probably a little more dangerous than I was aware of as it was actually going on. Certainly my sergeant major was in a real sweat as he watched the trespassers drive away. An example of ignorance being bliss on my part.

Six

In the evenings at the camp at Mirfa I would sit and talk with the men, doing my best to answer their questions. They would ask things like, 'How many camels has your father got?' and roar with laughter when I said none. In fact, as wealth was judged by the number of camels owned, I'm sure they didn't believe me.

I used to ask the words for things so I could improve my arabic vocabulary. On one occasion an enquiry revealed the less savoury side of their attitudes. We were at the coast and there were crabs on the shore. I said, 'What is that thing with eight legs scuttling along the ground?' One of the men replied, 'Yehudi' meaning Jews. They had an inbuilt hatred of the Jews, and anything that was monstrous they would describe as 'Yehudi'.

I said, 'How can that be? Have you ever met one? They're people just like you.' But no. They'd never seen them, never met them, never had anything to do with the Jewish people, but they regarded them as alien in every sense. I tried to reason with them about this but they didn't want to know. And of course Islam forbade them talking to infidels, and anyone not a Muslim is an infidel. They talked to me because I was in command and the sheiks had told them to respect my orders.

The Arabs I led, and all those I came into contact with, had many fine and noble qualities, but this incipient anti-semitism was hard to take.

Their strict adherence to Islam meant that the days had to be tailored to fit around the times of prayer. You might have an order to set off somewhere at 0630, but if 0630 was the time for them to get their prayer mats out and turn to Mecca, there was nothing to be done about it.

I was fascinated by Islam, as I am by religions generally. I even read parts of the Koran. I think that, like a lot of the great religions, the good side of it is splendid.

This business of having to build our timetable around prayers actually postponed our participation in the one little battle we had. Opposing groups laid claim to the Buriemi Oasis, which, as the only source of water for hundreds of miles, was a very valuable asset. We had the job of reclaiming it and generally calming things down. After prayers were over of course.

As battles go, it was a pretty strange one. The trouble was that the two sides were all dressed in civilian clothes and it was difficult to know who was who. But after we lobbed a few mortar shells over the heads of the combatants they simply surrendered. So the mission was a successful, if confusing one. Indeed, we later received a letter from Prime Minister Anthony Eden congratulating us all on the operation.

But there was a tragic postscript. The Bedouin are great coffee drinkers, and they would use anything metal to grind the beans with. One of them found an unexploded two-inch mortar bomb, which no doubt looked ideal for the job, with its little fin to hold on to and the blunt end.

He blew himself to pieces.

We were based on the edge of what's called the Rubal Khali, which means 'The Empty Quarter', where very few people had ever been. I used to go out into this area to sit and think. It was very peaceful in the cool of the evening, with the camp in the distance, to settle down and contemplate the direction my life was taking. I didn't know about meditation then, but the feeling of being totally at peace out there in the wilderness had a similar calming effect.

I suppose I've always been slightly nervous with people and never fully at ease in their company. But in the Rubal Khali, for the first time in my life I had a wonderful feeling of tranquillity. I pondered two questions during this time. What did I want to do with the rest of my life? And what did I feel about God and religion?

But I never made progress beyond a certain point. I felt peaceful, I felt at ease, but what I realised after a while was that I needed input or guidance. You need teachers at certain points in your life, and if ever I needed one I think that was the time. But none was available.

Animals were rare, so we had no meat, except an occasional goat which would be killed and cooked as a weekend treat. The cook at HQ Sharjah killed a goat early every Saturday morning. On one occasion he was found having sexual intercourse with it and was thrown into the army prison. He was most upset and indignant about this, saying that he had been doing it for years, thought it was a perk and couldn't understand what all the fuss was about. The rest of the time it was ghee, a sort of unrefined butter, and rice flavoured with basil. There was not much fresh fruit, but plenty of dates of course. This meant you had to be careful of scurvy, which was kept at bay by a meagre supply of vitamin pills, and cuts wouldn't heal very quickly. The main supplement to our diet came in tins – baked beans and tomato soup were particular favourites.

Occasionally the men would trap something like a jerboa – a small rodent – which would be cooked on a spit and eaten with great relish. There was also the odd rabbit, desert fox and, very rarely, a hyena.

Once, somebody brought me a jerboa that had turned up in a trap, and I decided to keep it as a pet in a rough wooden cage. The men thought this very odd indeed. Why didn't I eat it? Then one of them caught an owl with an injured wing. I kept him too; as he couldn't fly, he used to sit on the desk in my tent. One day when I was out the owl got into the cage and ate the jerboa.

Knowing I had this odd predilection for giving animals house room, it was only natural that when several of the Arabs found a desert fox with its paw in a trap, they should bring it to me. Desert foxes are smaller and much lighter in colour than ours, and this one had a really appealing face and quite lovely eyes. I made a lead for it out of wire, and a collar, woven round with cloth. It got to the point where he would sit on my knee and allow me to feed him.

This fox snarled and growled if anybody else came near him. One night I was woken up by this sound and staggered out, half asleep, to see what was going on. I found he'd got his lead caught around one of the tent lines and was almost strangling himself. As I released him he jumped up and bit my nose. He cut so deep, the end of my nose was literally hanging on a hinge of flesh.

As it happened, I doubled as the doctor for the squadron, and managed to find some penicillin powder. I think it was meant to make injections out of, but I sprinkled this on, got a roll of plaster and patched myself up as best I could.

Two days later I was pouring water out of a canvas bag into a glass when my hair stood on end like a dog. Oh my God, I thought, *rabies*. A little knowledge can be very dangerous, and the only thing I knew about rabies was that once the symptoms set in you were finished. And hydrophobia is one of the symptoms. There I was, miles from anywhere, in command of 140 men, with a painfully swollen nose and thinking I'd got rabies.

It was evening. I just dropped everything and walked out into the desert. I walked and walked and walked, and eventually slumped down and fell asleep. I woke up a few hours later, still absolutely convinced I'd got rabies.

We had radio contact with headquarters and I called the colonel and told him about the accident. 'Are you all right?' he said.

'Yes, I am okay really. I'm just a little worried about rabies.' A classic piece of British understatement.

'Oh, God! The nearest doctor is in Bahrain, and it will take at least four days to get him out to you.'

I said I thought I'd better see him.

So I had an anxious four-day wait. This doctor was flown down to Sharjah. He drove in a Land Rover towards me and I drove towards him. We met at an intermediary point out in the desert. He had a look at my wound and said, 'You stuck it up pretty well. It should have been stitched, of course, but you seem to have got it just about right.'

'What about . . . rabies?' I asked.

'Oh, no chance. The foxes out here are so clean because they're away from civilisation. They don't have any of these nasty diseases.'

I was so relieved I could have kissed him.

And I forgave the fox, of course.

Every three months or so we moved our squadron to another outpost. For some reason I couldn't take the fox with me on our next move and offered him to the incoming captain. He was quite intrigued and readily agreed. It would be nice to say that was the end of the story, but I later heard that the fox also bit his new owner, who promptly shot him. So that was the end of him, I'm afraid. I got on very well with the Arabs and was accepted by them. I was lucky that there was no sign of Islamic fundamentalism or Saddam Hussein at the time.

Just under two years after I had stepped off the ship at Port Said my posting in the Gulf came to an end. I left for home on 7th December, 1956.

The whole experience was very rewarding but also quite

strange. I'd had two years leading an almost biblical existence, and felt as if I'd got into my hosts' ways.

I arrived back in England completely disorientated. The
country of my birth seemed like another planet. I stayed for
a few days in an hotel in London, near Victoria station, and
the traffic, noise and people nearly drove me insane. I wanted
to go straight back to the Gulf. I thought I would never, *ever*
be able to readjust. The busyness and bustle was awful.

This peculiar, not-quite-here state persisted after I arrived
home for leave. By this time my parents had moved out
of Rutland House and to a bungalow they'd had specially built in a village called Trowell, between Ilkeston
and Nottingham.

I was due to get my discharge papers by this time and rang
the War Office to remind them that during my two years in
the Gulf I'd had no leave. They got round this in an unusual
way. I was re-enlisted in the Army for a further four months
to give me all the leave I was entitled to. This effectively made
me a civilian with four months' pay in my pocket.

Here I was, twenty-five years old, an ex-Army captain
with no particular qualifications, still undecided as to what
to do with the rest of my life. And in an incredible state of
bewilderment.

Inadvertently, I hit upon a form of physical therapy. I threw
myself into building a garden shed. I laid the concrete floor,
built and erected the wooden framework, put up the walls and
roof, added the windows and door. I wired it for electricity,
plumbed in water and leaded the hut where it connected up
with the house. I spent my whole time building this shed,
which is still standing today.

During all this, my father became very ill. For a while we
really thought he might be dying. He went into hospital to
have some tests and they found he was diabetic. Then they
discovered two TB spots on his lungs. So he had to take early
retirement, at only fifty-five. But much to our relief he began
to make a recovery. Medication cleared up the TB, his insulin

balance was put right and eventually he was able to resume a perfectly normal life.

So I stayed at home for six months building this shed, and coming down, as it were, from the high of having lived in the Persian Gulf. I think to some extent I've never got over it.

I'd always wanted to act, particularly in films, and thought I would now explore the possibilities in earnest. I was pondering how to do this when a letter arrived from a man named Huffner who ran a company called Oriental Carpet Manufacturers, just next to the Old Bailey in London. He said my name had been given to him by someone I served with in the Gulf. Would I be interested in going for an interview with a view to being the company's agent in Tehran? He wanted someone with my experience to go out into the desert and collect carpets from some of the nomadic peoples there. This sounded fascinating.

The interview with Mr Huffner went well and I was offered a job. But the job was initially in their London warehouse, in order for me to learn about the carpet business. The other condition was that I had to learn Persian. So part of my time would be taken up attending a course at the Berlitz language school. After which, if all went well, I would be sent out to Persia as their agent. I agreed and was put on a six-month trial period.

I must say, it really was fascinating learning about the different styles and patterns of Persian carpets. One piece of knowledge I picked up was that if you rubbed a carpet with a damp cloth and any dye came off, it had been patched-up. Shortly after this an American couple came in and I was allowed to show them the stock.

'There's one test we always do,' I told them, anxious to show off what little I knew. I took my handkerchief, wet it, and rubbed the corner of a rug they were looking at.

'Oh look,' I exclaimed in a very knowing way, 'a bit of dye's come off here. That's no good, is it?'

I saw two of the salesmen glowering at me. I had talked

the couple out of the extremely expensive item they had come to buy. They were so grateful they invited me to dinner that evening.

My employer was less enchanted.

In all honesty, things were not working out too well with Oriental Carpet Manufacturers. I was no good as a salesman, and on one memorable afternoon I was found asleep on a pile of rugs in the storeroom. And it was about this time that the Persians nationalised their carpet industry, so the role I was going to play over there disappeared anyway. It was with honour that we decided I wouldn't carry on with them. If I had taken the job and stayed I would have seen the overthrow of the Shah and the arrival of Ayatollah Khomeini.

I was living in a bedsit in Earl's Court while working in London; not much more than a cubby-hole with a wash basin and a bed in it. I also had an old gramophone and was catching up with rock 'n' roll, the advent of which had passed me by while I was out in the Gulf. Most evenings would be spent listening to Pat Boone and Johnny Ray records.

The bedsit existence was not nice. I can understand the loneliness and unhappiness that can ensue from living in one. I used to walk down to Earls Court station, where there was a stall selling tea and sandwiches, just to have somewhere to go. I had no friends. And my only real social contact came when I visited my parents and girlfriend, Kath, at the weekends. I was still in this mixed-up state of not knowing what I wanted or what I was going to do.

The desire to act, particularly in films, grew stronger and stronger. I used to go to the cinema a lot, and after every film I'd write down the name of the director and the production company from the end credits. When I got back to the bedsit I would send them a letter asking for work. I must have written hundreds of these letters. If I got a reply at all, it would be from a casting director saying, 'Sorry, nothing available at the moment'.

Then one day, I received a telegram from the director Brian Desmond Hurst asking me to go to his mews house in Belgravia.

I was shown into a long room whose walls were covered with paintings. Very expensive statues and a profusion of *objects d'art* were scattered everywhere. At the far end, sitting in a massive chair behind an ornate antique desk, was Brian Desmond Hurst. He was a big man, both physically and in personality.

'Come in, come in, sit down. I've got this letter here from you.' I sat down and he said, 'Tell me more about yourself.'

When I'd given him a brief résumé, with only a little exaggeration about my acting track-record, he said, 'Right,' and picked up the telephone. He gave a few details about me to whoever was at the other end then handed the phone to me.

'William Roache?'

'Yes, hello.'

'Right. The film starts shooting on Monday at Shepperton. We pay forty pounds a day, will that be all right?'

Of course that sounded absolutely wonderful to me and I said, 'Yes.'

'It's probably only about three or four days' work,' the voice continued. 'And you are a member of Equity, aren't you?'

I heard myself say, 'Yes, of course.' Because I knew if I said I wasn't that would be the end of my film career.

Mr Hurst then took the phone from me, put it down and said, 'Right, you've got the part. Now, I don't mind telling you I'd like to go to bed with you. But don't worry about it. I never force myself on anybody.'

My jaw dropped and I stared at him.

'Don't make up your mind now,' he said. 'It's open house here every evening; you're very welcome to come along and meet some famous people. Off you go now, and I'll see you on Monday for the filming.'

I walked out of there in a daze. I'd got a film part, lied about being in Equity and been propositioned for the first time in my life.

It was an extraordinary day.

Later, I actually went to a couple of his parties, and they were very good; I remember meeting the actress Janet Munroe at one of them. I also discovered that Brian Desmond Hurst was a cousin of the renowned American film director John Ford. As for his proposition, it was never mentioned again, and you were all right as long as you made sure you weren't the last one to leave.

But my big fear as I walked away from his flat that Wednesday – five days before the film was due to begin shooting – was what I was going to do about Equity membership. Equity was a very closed shop. I had visions of the whole film being blacked and me being thrown off the set.

When the contract came through the post a couple of days later, I decided that honesty was the best policy. I went to the Equity office, at number 8 Harley Street, convinced they would show me the door. My acting career was going to start and end with one unfulfilled contract, I was sure of it.

But when I got there and showed them the contract the official I spoke to just said, 'Oh yes, fine, here you are,' and handed me a membership card. Almost always you start with Equity as a temporary member. But he made me a full member on the spot. By an incredible stroke of luck I had crashed straight in.

The film was *Behind the Mask*, based on John Hunter's exciting novel *The Pack*, and it starred Michael Redgrave. Vanessa Redgrave was in it too and she had one line. I had two. It was a drama about doctors; the title referring to the green mask of the surgeon. Tony Britton, Ian Bannen and Lionel Jeffries were also in it.

I played a young doctor in a scene where three of us were waiting to be interviewed for a job as a hospital anaesthetist.

Someone came out to the waiting room, I exchanged a few words with him, then went through a set of swing doors to have my interview. Apart from having to turn up the following day for some shots where I was in the background, that was it.

Mr Hurst's only real contribution was to tell me to wear a blue suit and be sure to get a haircut.

I don't think it was a particularly good film, but it was my first real acting job. I had seen professional actors at work and gained some insight into how a studio functioned.

I was extremely grateful to Brian Desmond Hurst for giving me that first break. But I found later that you never mentioned you had made a film for him, because it was automatically assumed you had got it for the wrong reasons.

Seven

Inspired by my film debut, I renewed my efforts to find more work by making myself write a hundred letters a week to casting directors. On average, I received fifty or sixty replies, most of them saying, 'Sorry, nothing doing.' But seven or eight might lead to interviews.

One of these was with the casting director at Beaconsfield Studios, and he gave me a small part in the television series *Ivanhoe*, starring Roger Moore.

I arrived at Beaconsfield at 8.00 a.m. on the appointed day and was issued with knitted string leggings, vest and balaclava helmet – all painted silver to look like armour. Then I was given a bow and quiver of arrows. Roger Moore, his hair in curlers, came along and introduced himself, and he was very friendly. He proved to be a great practical joker, always fooling around and doing things like shoving arrows into people's bottoms as they were trying to do their scenes. It was great fun.

Then my name was called and I was told to climb on to the battlements. These were made of wood, indeed the whole castle front was made of wood, and the sole camera was down on the ground.

'Right!' the director shouted. 'Have you got your script?'

'Yes!' I called back.

'Well, forget about that. It's all different. What I want you to do is look out to the front, then turn around and shout behind you, 'My Lord, a knight is coming and he rides alone!' Then I want you to look to the front again, take an arrow out of your quiver, string it, point it and say, 'Dismount, sir knight! And keep to the path!' Have you got that?'

'Uhm, well, er . . .'

'Good! You don't want any rehearsal, do you? Action!'

I thought, What the hell do I do? Oh yes. Look to the front, then turn around. 'My Lord, a knight is coming and he rides alone!' Now what? Yes: look to the front again. Take an arrow out of the quiver, string it, point it. 'Dismount, sir knight! And keep to the path!'

At which point the director yelled, 'Cut! Well done! On to the next scene!'

I hadn't a *clue* what it had been like, and suspected it was absolutely dreadful.

I stayed around to watch the shoot, all of which was undertaken at the same breakneck speed and without rehearsal. A little later the director came to me and said, 'Ah, Roache. Just get up on the battlements again, lean over and look to the right of camera for about ten seconds, will you?

'Ready? Action!'

I looked to the right of the camera and began dutifully to count to ten.

'Cut!'

Clambering down, I asked him what I was supposed to be doing.

'You were watching prisoners being tortured,' he said.

Great! I thought. You tell me after the event. There was no time to actually *act* anything.

That was the only episode of *Ivanhoe* I filmed, but it was far from being the only one I appeared in. Whenever they had a scene with a sentry standing on the battlements with a bow it was me up there. They used it a lot and I should have had repeat fees, but never did. It always amused me to watch the series on TV knowing the actors hadn't an inkling as to what they were supposed to be doing.

My letters to casting directors garnered me another small film part, in *The Queen's Guards*, directed by Michael Powell. My scene was set in a tent in the desert, oddly enough, and I played a wireless operator. This involved a couple of lines of dialogue. Then there were a few scenes in which I appeared in the background. Again, I stayed after my bit was done in order to observe and learn.

I watched a scene in which two British actors played an Army officer and an Arab sheik. It was a tricky scene in that they were supposed to be enemies, yet they admired and respected each other. They were friends, sort of, and were saying goodbye for the last time. The whole thing amounted to just three or four lines of dialogue. It was rehearsed with the assistant director and then Michael Powell came out of his caravan at the back of the studio to shoot it.

'Let's go for it then,' he said. 'Action!'

They went into the scene and the actor playing the Arab dried up. So Mr Powell told the assistant director to get them sorted out and went back into his caravan. They went through it, Michael Powell reappeared and the actor dried again. When this happened a third time, the actor said, 'I'm sorry, Mr Powell, but I've got a thing about this line'.

'A thing?' Michael Powell said. 'I don't pay you to have a *thing* about your lines! Get it right or you're out!' Then he turned on his heel and went back to his caravan. After quite a number of takes they finally got through it.

I didn't like that, and wouldn't have wanted to work that way myself. The actor had a scene that was obviously difficult and I felt he wasn't being supported. Of course, it could be that Michael Powell was a good psychologist and this particular actor needed that sort of treatment. But I've found that most actors are sensitive people who respond to encouragement and nearly always need reassurance. If directors do this they can bring out the best in you.

I was a little surprised and a bit uncomfortable about the incident.

I was beginning to gain an insight into the art of acting by this time. I realised that if I was lucky enough to have a big opportunity come my way I wouldn't have the skill and experience to fully exploit it. It's one thing to have an opportunity, quite another to use it in a way that takes you forward. It seemed to me the best place to learn the basic craft of acting was in the theatre before a live audience. So I started writing to theatrical companies.

When I heard auditions were being held for West End plays I went along to read for them. I did one with Albert Finney, for a small part in *Billy Liar*, and found him a very strong and likeable character. While I was reading for that part I could feel I wasn't right. It confirmed I wasn't really ready yet, and needed to clock up stage experience.

I took some private lessons from a woman called Ellen Pollack, who was a quite well-known actress at the time. I went along to her house for a couple of hours a week and she instructed me in audition pieces and basic stagecraft. That was very helpful.

I was also writing to agents. One of the leading ones was St James Management, run by Laurence Olivier. I didn't have an address for them, but I knew he was appearing at the Cambridge Theatre in *The Entertainer*, so I wrote to him there, expecting him to pass the letter on.

Much to my surprise, and immense pleasure, I got a short note from Sir Laurence himself saying, 'Come to the stage door and I'll see you for a few minutes. Be there at 7.10.' So of course I was outside the door at 7.00 p.m. sharp. Seven-ten came and went. No Sir Laurence. I thought, well, why should he remember?

At 7.15 he suddenly strode around the corner and straight up to me. 'Mr Roache?' he said. 'Do come in.' I followed him to his dressing room. He gave me a gin and tonic, and offered me a cigarette – an 'Olivier', naturally – and said, 'I hope you don't mind me getting ready while we're talking.' Then he proceeded to put on his make-up and sort out his wardrobe.

He chatted away about his gout, and how he was shortly off to Hollywood to make *The Prince and the Showgirl*, with Marilyn Monroe. During our talk the door opened and that wonderful old actor George Ralph looked in. 'This is Mr Roache,' Sir Laurence said, introducing me as though I were a colleague of equal standing. That made me feel absolutely fabulous. Here I was, sitting in the dressing room of the country's most celebrated living actor, and he had put me totally at ease.

Eventually he said, 'What can I do for you?'

'Well, I've come into acting rather late,' I explained. I was twenty-five at this time. 'Most of the other actors I've spoken to say I should get out and find a more secure profession. I just thought a word of advice from you would be worth a hundred from anybody else.'

He said, 'Don't give up, that's all I can tell you. I had two years myself that were absolutely terrible, with nothing happening at all. It was really dreadful. But if it's in you, keep at it.

'I'm going to America after this,' he added, 'but when I get back, write to me, remind me about this conversation and I'll see what I can do for you.' Then he shook my hand and wished me luck. I walked out of there completely rejuvenated and determined to carry on. I was thrilled to bits that he should be so kind and generous to a young unknown.

That meeting made me realise – and this has been confirmed many times since – that truly great people will always find time for you, and make you feel during that time that you are the most important person in the world.

There is a nice little sequel to this story. I never did write to Sir Laurence as he suggested. I wanted to, just to thank him, but was wary of seeming to be a boot-licker or a sycophant. But many years later, in the 1970s, he came to the Granada studios to film *Cat On a Hot Tin Roof* with Robert Wagner and Natalie Wood, *King Lear* and a play with Joanne Woodward. I was in the corridor one day making a telephone call, and as I finished someone behind me said, 'Hello. I'd just like to say how much I enjoy you in *Coronation Street*.'

I turned round to find Laurence Olivier standing in front of me.

'Oh,' I said, 'I'm *so* pleased to have met you. I've got a story to tell you.'

I walked up the corridor with him and recounted how we had met twenty years before, and how encouraging and kind he had been. When I finished he looked at me and there were tears in his eyes. He said, 'What a wonderful story.'

'It was a wonderful time,' I responded. 'You gave me the will to go on and are responsible for me being here now.'

'Well, we're going to be seeing a lot of each other, aren't we?' he said. 'Because I'm here for a while.' And he talked about all the other actors who were going to be in those television plays he was doing – Robert Wagner, Natalie Wood, and so on. He was quite frail by then, but he still generated this tremendous warmth. I wanted to put my arm around him.

Olivier was a great *Coronation Street* fan, and he had the ambition to appear in it. As a matter of fact, negotiations started for him to play a cameo, and some work was done on a script. Sadly, it didn't happen, I think because his health became too bad. It is one of the more intriguing 'might-have-beens' in the Street's history.

I came away from that first meeting with Sir Laurence absolutely determined to crack on with acting in a proper way. It was no good doing bits in films and hanging around. Theatre was the only thing. I went straight to the office of an agent called Daphne Scorer. It wasn't a big-time agency, and you didn't have to be signed-up with her; anyone could drop in and see what was going.

I told her a pack of lies. I said I'd been in repertory in Colwyn Bay. When I was at Rydal school I knew the rep, and remembered the names of some of the actors there, so was able to fib convincingly. I don't like lying. I don't approve of it at all really, but I felt I had to break this mould, as I had when I pretended to be in Equity.

Two days later Daphne Scorer asked me back to her office. I sat there while she told a producer called Norris Staton what a wonderful young actor I was, and about all the parts I'd played in Colwyn Bay. He turned to me and said, 'I'm doing a summer season at Clacton for twelve weeks. Would you like to come along as juvenile lead?'

We shook hands and signed the contract on the spot.

Outside, I panicked. I had never been in the professional theatre and my acting experience amounted to schoolboy plays and a handful of tiny parts in films and TV. Now I was supposed to manage juvenile lead in a summer season at Clacton-on-Sea.

The company was called The Unicorn Players, and we rehearsed in London under the director, Donald Masters. Clacton town hall was to be our venue and the first play was a terrible thriller called *The Last Mrs Murdoch*.

At the rehearsal, the other actors used terms like 'upstage', 'downstage', 'corpsing', 'downstage right' and 'floats'. I hadn't the faintest idea what they were talking about. But I worked as hard as I could and got through it somehow. Although there was one uncomfortable moment when Donald Masters shouted from the stalls, 'I can't hear anybody except Roache! And I don't particularly want to hear him!'

I wasn't very good in that first play, and in the second I was given a much smaller part. But I was working. And people were being helpful. By the third play I began to get a bit of confidence and to know what I was doing. I was starting to develop. I remember Donald Masters saying to me, 'I've never seen anybody improve so much'.

Summer seasons have a sort of holiday feel about them.

We rehearsed in the morning, had the afternoon free, and performed in the evening. So on nice days you could sit on the beach while you learnt your lines. You always had a book in your hand because you were doing a play a week.

I stayed in a small bed and breakfast place not far from the theatre. One of the girls from the company was in a room upstairs and she was having an affair with one of the other actors. The owners didn't like this and they started laying traps to stop him coming in. They put empty tin cans around outside at night so he'd kick them over when he entered. I managed to warn him about those. However, the lovers were discovered and there were tears at breakfast one day when she was told to leave.

We were a very happy company. At the end of the twelve weeks we had become a very intimate group, and couldn't believe our little world would ever end. But of course it did. We even decided to have a reunion in London but sadly, rather like a holiday romance, by then we'd all picked up different threads and were moving off in different directions. After a couple of hours of reminiscing, no further contacts were kept up. But it was an important learning experience for me.

Arriving home, I found a letter I had written to Nottingham rep, at that time run by a man called Val May, had been answered. They were offering me a job as an ASM – assistant stage manager – which involves shifting the scenery, sweeping the stage and, if you were lucky, one or two roles. The pay was £6.10.0d a week.

Nottingham was a theatre with great prestige and I jumped at it. An added bonus was that I could live at home because my parents' bungalow was only fifteen minutes away. And it was a fortnightly company – they changed the plays every two weeks. A wonderful indulgence.

But it was quite different being a stage manager. There was a lot of menial work involved and I had to address members of the cast formally. There were two ASMs apart from me – Norman Florence, and Brian Blessed, with whom I was to begin a lifelong friendship. The three of us shared a little place next to the boiler room where there were piles of coke. I had a permanent sore throat from the fumes there.

One of the first plays staged while I was there was *Hamlet*, in which I took ten or twelve minor parts. The Canadian actor Donald Sutherland, just beginning his career at that time, was in this production. We followed it with a well-received version of *Peer Gynt*.

When you do period plays you nearly always have to wear a wig, and the ideal is to have a wig block made to the shape of your head. My fellow ASM, Norman Florence, wanted a personalised wig block and decided to make his own. He set about this one afternoon when he was alone in the theatre, pouring plaster of Paris over his head to make a mould.

Inexperienced at this kind of work, and probably having overestimated the amount of plaster necessary, he was horrified to find it setting almost instantly. And he had given little thought as to how he was going to breathe. We came back to find him looking like the 'Man in the Iron Mask', rushing around banging his head against the walls trying to get the thing off. He could have done something really horrible to himself. But that didn't stop us all falling about with laughter.

You could call Norman's little mishap a case of real stage fright. In fact, stage fright is something actors don't really talk about; the expression is considered inappropriate. But I have witnessed actors petrified with fear during productions. On one occasion, I saw someone freeze with their hand on a door knob and unable to move. Only once have I seen an actor stricken with this kind of thing while still in the wings. His cue had passed and he couldn't move. We had to carry him on in the end.

But we *all* get nervous. Any actor who doesn't isn't worth his salt. And the better known you become, the greater the feeling of nerves. As it gets nearer and nearer to curtain-up, the more you feel you're not going to be able to do anything. But the minute it starts, you get into it, you hear your own voice speaking and you enjoy it. Acting is an incredibly difficult thing. Trying to concentrate on anything for two hours without deviating is not easy.

Even now, in *Coronation Street*, when they say, 'We're going for a take. Quiet studio. Ready, action!' your nerves start. If there's just two of you doing a scene, you've got the whole studio – sound, vision-mixers, producers, directors – watching. Over forty people who can only operate if you're working. If you stop, the system stops. You can't be doing that and not be nervous. But I think the day you don't feel nervous is probably the day you should pack it in.

I remember seeing John Gielgud and Ralph Richardson in the make-up room at Granada once – they were doing a Pinter play – and Gielgud said, 'I'm as nervous as a kitten, Ralphie, nervous as a kitten.' I thought it was lovely to hear these theatrical greats talking about being nervous. But it's only natural. You're bound to feel nervous.

After Nottingham I continued sending out letters. One of them brought an invitation from Oldham rep to audition for juvenile lead. Oldham, although a weekly rep, operated twelve months a year, and it also had an excellent reputation. Among actors, who tend to be a superstitious lot, it was considered a lucky place.

Brian Blessed, who had been to Bristol Old Vic drama school, helped me prepare for my audition. He worked very hard on me and his contribution was extremely positive. So when I got the Oldham job, at eight pounds a week, it was partly thanks to Brian.

The theatre at that time was run by Harry Lomax, who had been there for many years, but not long after I joined he was replaced by a man called Carl Paulsen. There was a big to do about this. There were protests, demonstrations and marches through the streets with banners. But all to no avail. Not that any of this reflected on Carl Paulsen, who was very sharp and hard working, if a little waspish and low on tolerance of anyone who didn't pull their weight.

In my first week I appeared in *Tea and Sympathy*, which was about American college boys, and it proved very popular. But something very disturbing occurred one afternoon. I had gone to the prop room and got talking to the man who made the scenery. He had been in a prisoner of war camp and I found his story fascinating. Consequently, I was late on stage to hear the director's notes.

After notes, an actor called Geoffrey Atkinson announced that seventeen pounds, collected as Equity dues, had been stolen from his jacket pocket. The management rang the police and we were told they would be along in half an hour. I thought I'd spend the time having a cup of tea and a cheese roll at the café opposite. What I hadn't heard was that no one was to leave the theatre.

When I got back the police were there interviewing everyone. I was just in time to see a female ASM asking one of the officers if she could speak to him in private as she had something to say. My interview was left to last, and when I was called into the office one of the policemen said, 'You're new here, I gather.'

'Yes, I am.'

'I understand you left the theatre when you heard the money had been taken.'

'Yes, I popped across the road for a snack.'

'Didn't you know nobody was supposed to leave the theatre?

This was news to me and I said so.

'I gather you were late for notes,' he went on. 'When everybody else was on stage, you weren't there?'

'Yes, I was talking to the man in the scenery department.'

'And you don't deny you left the theatre afterwards?'

'No, of course I don't deny it.'

'Look,' he said, 'someone's told us they think you took

the money. Why not confess now and make it easier on yourself?'

I was dumbstruck. After a moment I managed to say, 'No, there isn't anything to confess. I didn't take the money.'

'Okay,' he sighed, 'we'll leave it for now. But I'd like you to come along to the station tomorrow.'

I spent the rest of that day terribly depressed and nervous. The following afternoon I reported to the station for a further interview, this time conducted by two CID men.

The one who did most of the talking didn't beat about the bush. 'If you confess,' he began, 'don't worry. It's no great thing. You probably won't lose your job.'

'I'm absolutely horrified by this,' I said. 'This job means a lot to me. If I was going to steal, which I wouldn't because it's not in my nature, I certainly wouldn't risk my job for seventeen pounds.' And I stamped out.

As it happens, that was the last I heard of the matter from the police. But Geoffrey Atkinson wouldn't talk to me. In the event he left after a few weeks, but he was quite convinced I'd done it. I felt one or two other people did too. It was the most awful feeling.

About two years after I left Oldham, an ex-caretaker was caught stealing from the dressing rooms. He knew the theatre's routine, and that on Monday afternoons the whole company would be on stage taking director's notes. Eventually he confessed to a whole string of thefts, including the one I was accused of.

But at the time the affair made my start at Oldham a very unpleasant one. I was innocent but I felt I was under a cloud of suspicion. And there's nothing I could do except carry on. The first couple of weeks were the worst, but as time went by, and new faces replaced the old, it eased off considerably.

There were lighthearted moments too. We were doing a play, the name of which I forget, in which the actor Henry Livings played a mayor. Henry is better known as a writer and he often talked about the art of ad libbing. In one scene he had to conduct the town band. At the end of that scene the curtain came down and there was a very quick change. I had to go on stage with an actress and play a quick love scene with her on the same set. We had to be ready because when the curtain dropped, Henry shot off and we shot on.

I was upstairs in the wardrobe department ferreting out clothes for the following week and told the ASM girl at the bottom to give me a shout when Henry got towards the end of his scene. I'm a bit hard of hearing, as I said, and when I heard, 'Bill! Bill! Quickly, you're on!' – or *thought* I heard it – I shot down the stairs. I couldn't see from the wings if the curtain was down; I assumed it was. Henry was standing on stage but I thought he'd just finished. So I ran straight on to the stage and to my horror saw the audience behind him. He was still doing his scene.

He looked at me and I looked at him. There was an awful pause. The audience didn't know what was going on. This was the moment for a great ad lib. I said, 'Sorry, Henry' and ran off again. Of course, the audience fell about. Then the curtain dropped and it came up again with me doing my next scene. With great difficulty.

Another time, again with Henry Livings, we did a play called *Death and Brown Windsor*, which was like a bad Agatha Christie. It was an *awful* play. It was all plot, times, dates and red herrings, and dreadful to learn.

The play started with Henry and myself sitting on a sofa, facing out front and having a conversation. Now, this play finished, three acts later, with Henry and me back on that sofa having another conversation. But in the opening scene, we found ourselves going straight into the end of the play. Ad-libbing madly, we tried to get back. Henry fed me a line. I couldn't pick it up. I tried a line. *He* couldn't pick it up. Because this play was all plot you couldn't just chat your way through it the way you could in other things.

So we sat there looking out front, sweat breaking out on our foreheads, facing the audience and totally lost. I shouted for the prompter and a plaintive voice from the prompt corner said, 'You jumped and I tried to follow you and I lost the place.' Everybody fell about. Then the prompter came on stage and we all studied the script. The audience were laughing, which is always good because it means they're with you. We finally got it going again and it was all okay.

The one thing I'd always dreaded when I went into acting was that I should ever have to come on a stage holding a rose and singing a song. Singing is not one of my talents. So of course, Carl Paulsen decided to do a Victorian musical drama called *Meet Me By Moonlight*. And I had to come on stage holding a rose and singing a song. Fortunately, the girl I was singing to couldn't sing either. Once I got over the initial embarrassment I quite enjoyed it.

Reps always have a pantomime at Christmas and *Robin Hood* was chosen the year I was at Oldham. Robin Hood is usually played by a principal boy, but Carl Paulsen cast me, because I was quite slim and good-looking in those days. So there I was in Lincoln green, with the tights, boots and hat with a feather in it.

We had a chorus of little girls, taken from a local drama school, and the panto began with them dressed as singing pixies. Then a horn sounded and they cried, 'It's Robin! It's Robin!' as I came heroically down a staircase, centre stage. On the opening night all went well until my entrance. I appeared at the head of the stairs. I threw my arms back in greeting. The orchestra swelled.

Then I tripped and bumped down the staircase on my bottom.

Eight

In 1958, while I was still at Oldham, Granada Television
went on the air. Still having the habit of writing to people
for work, I dropped a line to the casting director there. He
interviewed me and the contact led to some modest parts.

At that time, Granada screened three series – *Skyport*,
Knight Errant and *Biggles* – and I appeared in all of them.
When I was in *Biggles* a funny thing happened. The director,
Chris McMaster, was known for his hustling and bustling.
He was full of energy and always anxious to be getting on
with things. He was a lovely man.

During the shooting of one of the episodes I was in, he
said to an assistant, 'I want Biggles flying over the Arctic.
Paint an area of the floor blue with a white ice-flow on it.
And I want an extra in a polar-bear skin. We'll knock that
off in the next couple of days.'

In due course, the wardrobe mistress came up to him
and said, 'Excuse me, Mr McMaster, the polar-bear skin's
arrived.'

'Oh, good,' he said. 'Get the extra in it, I can shoot the
scene now.'

'There is just one thing – '

'No, don't bother me. Get the extra in the polar-bear skin
and put him on the ice-flow. I'll run the camera over it in a
couple of minutes.'

'But Mr McMaster – '

'Just get it done!'

So they got the extra into the skin and put him on the ice-flow. The camera angle was set up, the lighting was adjusted, the sound balanced. Chris McMaster came over and took a peak through the lens. The polar bear had a black bow-tie and buttons down his front.

They had to scrub that one.

I was fitting in the Granada jobs on my days off from Oldham. But after twelve months in rep I had got to saturation point. I felt my brain couldn't take another line of dialogue. So I decided to make the break, get myself back to London and pick up where I left off.

No sooner had I arrived in town and got myself a flat – another bedsitter – when Granada rang offering me the part of an art student in *Knight Errant*. In those days I had quite long hair, well before the sixties fashion, and if ever they needed a student type, it would be a case of, 'Get that Roache chap from Oldham rep.'

I went up and played this art student, finishing in the evening at around ten o'clock. I had an interview the next morning at Pinewood studios so I caught the midnight train from Manchester station. Unshaven, and wearing a navy-blue polo-neck jumper with casual trousers, I got into the last carriage, which was one with tables between the seats. At the far end was what I assumed was a teacher with two or three senior girls, perhaps going on a holiday or something. I sat near the other end, feeling pretty tired.

The train set off and I read and dozed a bit. Then it pulled up somewhere in the south Midlands and this youngish, quite smartly dressed chap with a small case got on. Despite the carriage being almost empty, he sat opposite me. I was feeling tired and dirty, and grew un-comfortable as he sat there blankly staring at me. I tried talking but he didn't say anything. Eventually I decided to take a nap, and lay along the seat with my head facing the aisle.

I was just dozing off when something made me open my eyes. It was pitch black outside and the window opposite acted as a mirror. In it, I saw the reflection of this man with his hand raised, looking as though he was about to rabbit-punch my throat. I leapt up and grabbed his hand. His eyes were quite wild and I realised there was something wrong with him.

Not knowing what else to do, I started talking, rapidly, about anything that came into my head. I was absolutely petrified. Not to mention shattered. Eventually I got him to sit down. I noticed that my travelling bag was in the aisle towards the end of the carriage. Presumably my would-be assailant had taken it off the rack and tossed it there.

It was 4 o'clock in the morning by now, and after about a quarter of an hour, having got him reasonably quietened down, I said, 'I'm just going to pick up my bag.' It was like talking to a frightened animal. He watched me intently as I very slowly slid out of the seat. I picked my bag up and carried on along the aisle toward the man and girls. I said, 'I've got a bit of a problem down there.' 'Yes, I think you have,' the chap agreed.

I walked on through to what I thought was the guard's van, but the door was locked. So I did what I've always wanted to do. I went into the loo and pulled the communication cord.

Nothing happened.

I pulled it again. And again. I hung on it. It unwound into a loop about nine inches long. Still nothing happened.

After about ten minutes the train ground to a halt. I expected the crunch of gravel as people ran to help. Nothing.

I went out of the loo and dropped the window in the corridor. The guard was leaning out of his window, next to mine.

'Did you pull the communication cord?' he said.

'Yes.'

'Right, you're for it! Twenty-five pound fine!'

'Just a second – '

'You're for it. We're coming into Luton in a minute. There's going to be the station master and a policeman there. Twenty-five pound fine!'

And he pulled his window up.

It was just beginning to get light, and sure enough, about five minutes later, we pulled into Luton. There, on a totally empty platform, was the station master and a policeman. They came in. The guard appeared, pointed at me, and said, 'That's him! That's the man!'

'What's all this?' the policeman said.

I nodded toward my attacker at the far end of the carriage, sitting quietly, looking very smart in his suit and tie. 'That man attempted to assault me,' I said.

The policeman looked me up and down. 'Oh, he did, did he?'

He walked along to the man and said very politely, 'Excuse me, sir. I'm terribly sorry, but a complaint has been made. I have to ask you to step off the train please.' The chap picked up his bag and meekly obeyed.

Then it was my turn. 'You, off!' the policeman barked.

So I got off the train and watched it pull away, carrying my only witnesses. As it disappeared down the platform the guard stuck his head out of the window and shouted, 'You're for it now! Twenty-five pound fine!'

I stood on that platform, looking and feeling like nothing on earth, facing a hostile policeman, a disgruntled station master and an extremely respectable looking young man who a short time before had come within seconds of pummelling me senseless. What could I say?

Before I had a chance, the man dropped his case and lunged at me. He got his hands around my throat and started screaming that I was a Russian spy.

The station master and policeman were frozen in shock for

a moment. Then they grabbed him. It took the three of us to manhandle him into the waiting room and hold him down until an ambulance arrived. Just before he was taken away, they opened his case and found it full of old railway tickets. I never found out what the story was, but I assumed the poor lad had escaped from an institution or something.

The policeman apologised to me and the station master said there was another train due in about half an hour. I was left on that desolate platform all by myself, completely drained.

I got to London with just enough time for a quick wash, shave and change of clothes, before catching another train to Pinewood. I staggered into the casting director's office looking and feeling a wreck.

'Ah yes, William Roache,' he said. 'We've met before, haven't we? Yes, I've got your particulars here. Great, jolly good, okay. Let you know if anything comes in.'

'Hold on,' I said. 'I've been to see you three or four times now. What do I need to get some work?'

'Quite frankly, you need a bit of luck.'

'Right,' I said, and told him about what happened on the train, concluding with, 'Don't you think I deserve a bit of luck?'

'Yes, I do,' he said, and gave me on the spot one line in Norman Wisdom's *The Bulldog Breed*.

I played a naval officer, making my appearance just before Norman Wisdom is sent up in a spaceship. I had to say, 'Fuel ducts at maximum pressure!' In a close-up, mind you. But if you blinked, you missed me. David Lodge, Robert Urquhart and Peter Jones were in it and, strangely, so was Johnny Briggs who plays Mike Baldwin. But we didn't meet. Years later, swapping stories about our careers, Johnny and I found we had been up for lots of the same films.

While I was doing *The Bulldog Breed* at Shepperton they were making *The Guns of Navarone* there, with Gregory Peck, Anthony Quinn, David Niven and James Robertson Justice. I was sitting in the canteen one day when Gregory Peck walked in. I couldn't believe my eyes. Talk about being star-struck! He was well over six foot, and a big man in every way, but elegant, with beautifully fine features. He took my breath away. If he'd been an accountant or a road sweeper, everyone would still have turned and looked. He had that kind of magnetism.

Then Anthony Quinn came along. He was kind of loud-mouthed and a little too brash for my tastes but, again, there was this incredible charisma and I was thrilled to see him. I've always loved meeting famous people, and I got a particular kick out of being in the presence of these two greats.

The next thing I got was a part in a film called *His and Hers*, with Terry Thomas. Curiously, the story concerned an English author who gets lost in the desert and is rescued by the Bedouin. When he gets back home he's been so influenced by their way of life he finds it hard to readjust!

The cast of *His and Hers* read like a roll-call of British comedy. Wilfrid Hyde White, Kenneth Williams, Joan Sims and Kenneth Connor were all in it. Janette Scott played the female lead and Oliver Reed had a tiny role.

My scene was set at London Airport. Terry Thomas was dressed in some sort of Arab headdress, and I was a reporter. I had to talk to him as we walked from his plane to the hangar. It was a scene of about two pages. And he was terribly keen. He wanted to go over and over and over this scene. He was very concerned to get it right. That wonderful Terry Thomas worried look was absolutely genuine.

When *His and Hers* was released, one critic called it the worst film of the year.

The pinnacle of television drama in those days was *Play of the Week*, which the various companies in the ITV network took turns making. It was highly prestigious and to be in it was really something. So I was absolutely thrilled to land the lead in one Granada was producing called *Marking Time*.

It was about a young British soldier in Germany who has

1 My parents, William and Hester Roache, pictured during the early years of their married life.

2 Rutland House, my birthplace in Ilkeston, Derbyshire.

3 A wartime photograph of my sister, Beryl, our mother and myself.

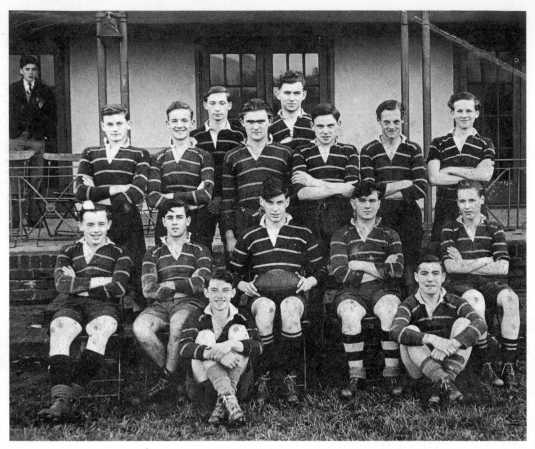

4 A proud member of the First XV rugby team at Rydal Senior School, Colwyn Bay, in 1946. I am sitting on the far right.

5 Me, at sixteen, in the garden of Rutland House with Patch, the dog.

6 Displaying the alligator I shot (twice!) during army service in British Guyana.

7 At the fort in the Buriemi Oasis in Trucial Oman. Note the dashing moustache.

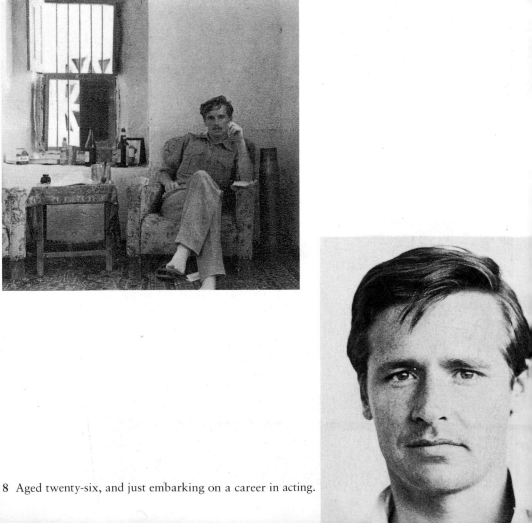

8 Aged twenty-six, and just embarking on a career in acting.

9 The cast of *Coronation Street* as of episode one, December 1960. *Back row, left to right:* Harry Hewitt (Ivan Beavis), Albert Tatlock (Jack Howarth), Ivan Cheveski (Ernst Walder), Dennis Tanner (Philip Lowrie), David Barlow (Alan Rothwell), Jack Walker (Arthur Leslie), an unnamed extra (William Croasdale), Frank Barlow (Frank Pemberton), Ida Barlow (Noel Dyson), Minnie Caldwell (Margot Bryant). *Front row:* Annie Walker (Doris Speed), Florrie Lindley (Betty Alberge), Linda Cheveski (Anne Cunningham), Elsie Tanner (Patricia Phoenix), Ena Sharples (Violet Carson), Christine Hardman (Christine Hargreaves), Kenneth Barlow (William Roache), an extra (Patricia Shakesby), an extra (Penny Davies), Martha Longhurst (Lynne Carol).

10 The five longest-running cast members celebrate the Street's eighteenth birthday in 1978. Jack Howarth, Doris Speed, Pat Phoenix, Violet Carson and I toast the future.

11 The turnout for Ken and Deirdre's screen wedding in 1981.

12 Doorstep confrontation: Ken and Mike shape up for one of the most gripping half hours in British television.

13 Will it be happily ever after for Wendy Crozier (played by Roberta Kerr) and Ken? In the end it was Wendy, not Mike, who led to the Barlow marriage breakup.

14 The Street's line-up in 1992, with the cast now well into three generations.

15 *Coronation Street* fan John Betjeman visits Granada Studios. Sadly, he never realised his ambition to appear in the programme.

16 The Queen and Prince Philip open Granada's new purpose-built Street set. Her Majesty became so engrossed in chatting to us all that the visit overran by half an hour.

17 Is Mike Baldwin about to clock Ken? Deadly rivals on-screen, in real life Johnny Briggs and I are the best of friends.

18 Nice legs, pity about the face. Yes, it's me, dragged-up for my part in John Bowen's *Disorderly Women* at the Hampstead Theatre in 1969.

19 Commentator Peter Alliss and Terry Wogan – fellow golf obsessives!

20 Celebrating summer solstice with the Druid Order at Stonehenge.

21 Margaret and Denis Thatcher welcome us to Downing Street shortly after the 1983 general election.

22 Sara and I were delighted when Betty Driver agreed to be our daughter Edwina's godmother. Here we are at the christening, with Verity and her godmother, Eileen Derbyshire.

23 Me, Verity and Kinky, the kinkajou which our family sponsors at Chester Zoo.

24 Posing for a portrait by renowned artist John Bratby R.A.

a relationship with a German girl and gets her pregnant. Alan Cook was the director, and we worked very hard on it together, rehearsing in London and subsequently recording up at Granada. I went back thinking, This is it. When the play comes out my career will really take off, and I will be ready.

I had an agent by that time and he said Granada wanted to talk to me about a series they were going to do. He thought it was a northern comedy serial, something rather like Norman Evans in *Over the Garden Wall*. I said I didn't want to do it. I was getting myself established in London, *Marking Time* was due to be aired in a few weeks and things were starting to look promising at last. 'You might as well go along for the interview, because there's nothing else on at the moment,' he said.

So, somewhat reluctantly, I went to the interview at the Granada offices. There were about half a dozen people there, including the producer and casting director. These occasions are usually quite frightening and you can find yourself shaking like a jelly. But I wasn't too bothered because I didn't particularly want the part.

I had a copy of the *Daily Telegraph* with me, and someone said, 'Just pick any article and read it, and go into Lancashire if you can.' We have no Lancashire accent at all in my family. But oddly enough, my mother, who was born there, used to go into a cod Lancashire accent and we would join in. It was a sort of silly, jokey thing. I found an article about the Liverpool MP Bessie Braddock flicking ink pellets at a political opponent. It was quite a funny piece and lent itself beautifully to the bit of broad Lancashire I read it in. Then they thanked me and I went home.

A couple of days later my agent rang and said, 'They liked you, and they want you to go up to Granada to do the pilot for the series.' A pilot is a trial episode made to assess the potential of a series. It helps management decide whether to go on and make more.

I said, 'There's no point. Even if I get it I really don't want to do it.'

'It's three days' work with all expenses paid,' he argued. 'You've got nothing else on, you might as well do it.'

I gave in and agreed. Without too much enthusiasm, to be honest.

The show was called *Florizel Street*.

As a matter of fact, Granada made two pilots, with two differing casts. In one, I played the young university student Kenneth Barlow. In the other, Ken was played by Philip Lowrie, who in the actual series portrayed Dennis Tanner, of course. Victor Tandy, who has since died, played Albert Tatlock. Most of the actors in the pilots, however, were the ones who would ultimately appear in the series proper. Doris Speed and Pat Phoenix, for example, were in both versions of the pilot.

I did my bit, and went back to London more or less convinced that was the last I would hear about *Florizel Street*. Then my agent rang again and said, 'They're going to try the series for a thirteen-week run and want you to play Ken Barlow'. I was still less than keen. But as he pointed out, 'To do thirteen weeks of a twice-weekly serial has got to be an even better shop window for you than *Marking Time*'. So I said, 'Okay, but I'm only doing the thirteen weeks'.

Granada decided to abandon the name *Florizel Street*. This was met with universal approval as everyone thought it sounded like a lavatory cleaner. The series was now to be called *Coronation Street*.

It turned out to be the longest thirteen weeks I have ever known.

Coronation Street was scheduled to begin on 9th December, 1960. There would be two episodes a week, at 7.00 p.m. on Mondays and Fridays. The Friday episode was live; Monday's was recorded, but as it couldn't be edited that was almost as nerve wracking.

A long and happy relationship with my colleagues, in both the management and cast, began on the very first day of rehearsals. And what a wonderful team they were.

I recall Jack Howarth coming up to me and saying, 'Hello, how are you?' and I asked whether he remembered meeting me at Rydal. He didn't at first, but it all came back when I reminded him about it.

I quickly grew to like Jack, and he was a joy to work with. A true professional of the old school, he was always a pillar of strength and faultless on his lines. He was sixty-five when *Coronation Street* started, when most people are retiring, and he died at eighty-eight, still working as hard as ever. Despite his somewhat gruff and abrasive Albert Tatlock persona, he was in fact a real delight. He loved telling rude stories, and invariably managed to get them wrong, but it was all part of the man's charm.

There was Violet Carson, the formidable Ena Sharples, an actress who combined great natural dignity and strength of character with a face you could break rocks on. She had a superb singing voice; if there was a piano around she would play and sing quite exquisitely.

I was always in awe of Vi, as was everyone; she had an air of authority that people respected her for. A perfect choice for Ena. If anything went wrong, she was the one who took the casts' grievances to management. But you didn't mess around with her. I admired Vi greatly, and liked her. I think she liked me too.

The show very soon established the most wonderful trio of characters in Ena, Martha and Minnie, the Gorgons of the Rovers' Return snug. Their characters meshed to make them a truly classic creation. Breaking them up by killing off Martha Longhurst was, I think, a mistake. Lynne Carol, who played Martha, was always very upset about it. She was bitter about having been written out.

She passed away only a couple of years ago. It was strange. The papers reported she had died of a heart attack while on holiday. It transpired this had been a mistake, so I wrote to her expressing my regret about the upset the misreporting must have caused her. But she had a real heart attack while my letter was in the post. It was sort of *déjà vu* in reverse; life following what had been written in the press. It was very weird.

And Margot Bryant – Minnie Caldwell – what a character *she* was. She'd sit there demurely, this little, frail, round-faced old dear with twinkling eyes, and yet she could come out with the most *horrendous* language. And she professed to hate children. Margot used to go into restaurants, ask to see the manager and throw her weight around a bit. I think she enjoyed shocking people. She would come out with the most outrageous statement then turn to you and wink. I remember asking her once what she would like to have been if she hadn't become an actress. 'A pirate,' she said. Her credo in life seemed to be simply to enjoy herself. She was great fun.

Sadly, towards the end, her memory started to go; in small ways at first – like calling her colleagues by their character's names – but it became increasingly problematic. There was an episode in which Jed Stone (Kenneth Cope), who lodged with Minnie and treated her like his mother, had to go to Liverpool. Everybody knew what that meant – Liverpool was synonymous with jail. At the end of the scene he gets into an unmarked police car and gives her a wave as he's driven off. Then Ena comes along and says, 'Where's he gone?'

'Liverpool,' Minnie says.

Knowing look from Ena.

End of episode.

At least that was the way it was supposed to go. When we came to film the scene, all went as planned until Ena walked up and asked where Jed was going. 'Birmingham,' Margot said.

It got a big laugh on set, of course, but it soon became apparent she was deteriorating. She had a flat in Brighton, and was once found wandering the streets, not knowing what was going on. It was quite heartrending. Eventually she had to go into a home, where she stayed for many, many years. Eileen Derbyshire was wonderfully caring, a true friend; she used to visit Margot regularly. I dropped in on one or two occasions but she barely recognised me. The last time I went she thought I was a doctor. But she was physically healthy and well looked after, so perhaps it was for the best. She died in 1987.

Margot was a lovely character. And I do mean *character*. I always thought she would have been marvellous as one of the spinster poisoners in *Arsenic and Old Lace*.

I remember dear old Frank Pemberton, who played Ken's father, with a great deal of affection. Frank was really dour, with his big, soft, cow eyes. He had this sort of comfortable, pipe-smoking exterior, but underneath he was a great worrier. In fact all of us were prone to tension in those early days of live broadcasts. One of the ways Frank and I handled this was by running through our lines during rehearsal in various accents – Scottish, Cockney and so on – or by reading them very fast or very slow. In every way imaginable, in fact, so that when we came to the real thing they were absolutely right.

In one early episode, Frank was particularly concerned about a certain line. The scene had us sitting at the breakfast table, so he wrote his dialogue on the boiled egg in front of him. But when you go out live, the adrenalin speeds up incredibly, and I watched as he smashed the egg before he got to the line. But it was all right, he got through.

Our characters always seemed to be at loggerheads, and these arguments usually grew out of the fact that Ken was at university, taking English and History, and his dad was a simple postman. Ken would get terribly upset about things like finding the sauce bottle on the table. In one such confrontation Frank had to say, 'I don't know anything about history except King Harold riding about on his horse with his hawk in his hand'. But on the night it came out as, 'I don't know anything about history except King Harold riding around on his hawk with his horse in his hand.' Only the sheer terror of live TV stopped us falling about over that one.

Frank had an old boat he kept moored in Jersey; it was actually used by John Huston to tow the rubber whale in *Moby Dick*. Between acting jobs, Frank would hire out this boat to take people on fishing trips. It sank during a storm, and somebody took it off him for salvage. He was deeply upset about that.

Alan Rothwell, who played Ken's brother, David, was with me at Oldham rep for a while. We were together in *Goodbye, Mr Chips*, in which he played one of the school-boys. I was very fond of Alan, and still am. We live not far from each other and he remains a great friend. When my wife Sara and I were married he acted as best man. One of the nice things about Alan is that he's just as fresh and bubbly a character now as when we were in rep.

Anne Reid was Ken's wife Val for the first nine years. Then she married Peter Eckersley and decided to go and do other things. We gave each other a little present when she left, and mine was a silver goblet with *We must do it again sometime* engraved on it. It's a memento I treasure. I'm pleased she went on to do so well in a variety of roles post-Street, particularly with Victoria Wood.

Noel Dyson, Ken's mum, was lovely; a real maternal figure. But she lived in London, and after a couple of years decided she didn't want the split life any more. She asked to leave, and being such a nice and good person the only way she could leave was to kill her off. So they had her run over by a 49 bus. We all wept as we sat and watched that.

It was an incredibly emotional scene, with the hearse driving off to the strains of the *Coronation Street* theme. That was one of the occasions that made me realise what a great theme it is. It's so flexible it somehow works for a funeral, a comedy scene, a piece of high drama – just about any situation you can think of. I've often noticed that a successful show tends to have a good signature tune. The theme tune for *Eastenders*, for instance, is terrific. But *Coronation Street*'s has really stood the test of time.

Arthur Leslie, who made Rovers' publican, Jack Walker, such a widely loved character, was the first real death we had on the Street. In so long-running a series it's inevitable that people are going to succumb to real illnesses and sometimes death, but knowing that in no way softened the tremendous blow of his passing.

He died quite suddenly of a heart attack while away on holiday. Again, as when Noel Dyson left, there was the terrible problem of what to do about the character. Obviously, you can't just ignore the fact that someone has disappeared. And usually the press has picked it up and everyone knows what has actually happened. So, with permission of the nearest relatives, the producers and writers devise a fitting exit for the character concerned.

Arthur was a genuinely warm, worldly wise and thoroughly laid-back character on screen and off. He had a long stage career before coming into the Street, and ran his own theatrical companies at various times. A very generous and kind person, albeit a man of few words. If I saw him sitting alone in the canteen, I would always go and join him. I like quiet meals, I'm not one for animated conversations at meal times, and Arthur was the best possible company. He was a comforting man to be with.

And what a wonderful match he and Annie (Doris Speed) were. Annie would be going off at the deep end about this, that and the other, and putting on airs and graces. And dear old Arthur would just say, 'Eeeh, Annie.'

What a balance you had there. Annie, the snob, always trying to be one up on everybody, constantly vying with the landlady (Mollie Sugden) at The Laughing Donkey; and Jack, just wanting to get on with running his pub and having a quiet life. They were brilliantly paired.

Having Kenneth Farrington play their son, Billy, was

another shrewd move on the part of the writers and producers. He was a very strong character in his own right and there was actually quite a subtle and complex interplay of relationships between him and Jack and Annie. The character definitely added to the Street's rich tapestry. Although having an actor called Ken playing someone called Billy, and a Bill playing someone called Ken occasionally caused confusion!

The next real death, after that of Arthur Leslie, was Graham Habberfield's. Another victim of a heart attack, Graham's demise was all the more tragic for him being only thirty-five years old. We were all numb with shock and terribly upset that such a young man should be snatched away so cruelly. He was so incredibly vital. The cast of a long-running series like *Coronation Street* grows into a kind of surrogate family, and any loss is deeply felt.

Graham, who played Jerry Booth, was a fine actor and, off screen, a very mercurial sort of guy. I felt a real affinity with him, if only because the pair of us had never grown up; we were always fooling around together and kidding each other. We would have mock sword fights in the corridor and devise practical jokes. One of Graham's favourite tricks, somewhat alarmingly, was to set fire to the newspaper you were reading!

One day, I was walking along a corridor at Granada and saw Graham dart around a corner at the far end. I knew he intended jumping out on me and decided to turn the tables on him. I ran up the corridor on tip-toe and pressed myself against the wall at the corner. I thought I'd give him a shock by swinging my foot around and catching him on the shin. This I did – quite gently, it wasn't a kick – and thudded into something soft. A great shout went up from Graham. He was down on all fours like a dog, ready to jump out on me, and my foot had caught him on the top of his eye, cutting it open.

I had to bundle him into a taxi and dash off to the hospital casualty department with him. And this was a Thursday afternoon, technical run-through day, when you simply have to be present. Of course the rumour went round the studio that we'd had a fight and Graham was much more badly hurt than he really was. Fortunately the hospital stitched him up and we were back in time, if somewhat breathless and red faced. Make-up had to be applied to the gash over his eye, but apart from that all was well.

I got on really well with Graham. He was an excellent colleague and a delightful conspirator in these kinds of japes. I missed him terribly.

Philip Lowrie was very good indeed as Dennis Tanner; I believe he was one of the best tragi-comic characters the Street has ever produced. All sorts of very funny, and occasionally touching, storylines were spun out from Dennis. It was a decided loss for the series when Philip decided to move on to other challenges.

Pat Phoenix, Dennis Tanner's mother, was one of *Coronation Street*'s most flamboyant, larger than life personalities. Pat was wonderfully lively, her sparkling eyes always full of fun and energy. She was very ambitious and saw herself, I think, as being very much in the mode of a 1930s film star. I intend nothing derogatory in saying this – I think she would have made a *smashing* thirties movie queen. She would have loved going out to meet people and would have given her all to the publicity. And when I say she was childlike, I mean in the sense of being open, outgoing and generous. None of which should be allowed to obscure the fact that she was an extremely good actress.

It's only true to say that she could also be very easily upset and a little temperamental at times.

In the Street's early days, around 1961 or 1962, there was a storyline where Ken's wife, Val, was unjustly accused of some kind of underhand behaviour. I can't recall if she was supposed to have stolen some money, or said something out of turn, but in any event Ena and Elsie ganged up on her. Ken confronted them, saying that if they uttered one more word on the subject he would take action. The scene ended with Ena and Elsie stunned into silence as Ken stormed out – a dramatic moment in which he put the pair in their place.

When we came to rehearse it, Pat said to the director, 'I don't think Elsie would take this from a young chap like Ken.' Some directors are very strong and insist we stick to the words as written, others are more flexible. The director at that time was one of the former and stood his ground. 'No,' Pat insisted, 'I don't think she would just stand there and let him say this to her.'

'Well,' I said, 'that's how the scene's written.'

Pat was adamant. 'No, no, I don't think so. At the end I want to say, "Oh, go on, get off!" or something.'

This annoyed me intensely, because the dramatic moment depended on finishing with a stunned silence. I could see it being watered down and that made me angry.

We rehearsed the scene and when we reached what should have been the silence at the end, Pat did indeed say, 'Oh, go on, get off!' I was absolutely furious. I never get temperamental at rehearsals, I prefer to discuss such differences of interpretation, but I could tell the moment was going to be ruined whatever the director or myself said.

Then, just before trying another run-through, Pat came up to me and said, 'Bill, at the end of this scene where I say, "Oh, go on, get off!" would you pause at the door? Because I'm going to pick up an ashtray and threaten to throw it at you.'

I snapped. 'No, I will not.' We had a blazing row in which we both said things we did not mean. I am pleased to say that this is the only row we ever had.

In the end, that scene was neither one thing nor the other. It was fudged and compromised, and completely lost its dramatic impact.

But as a result of this disagreement, Pat didn't talk to me for two years. We had occasionally to do scenes together, and those scenes would be done, but with no discussion, no running through lines before or after. There was simply no communication between us.

Two years later, on Pat's birthday, she announced a party at her house to which the whole cast was invited, except me. We were shooting an episode that afternoon. As we waited to make an entrance into the Rovers together she said, without looking at me, 'If you want, you can come tonight.' And I said, 'Thank you, Pat.' From that time on things were fine between us.

I'd hit something in her and she'd touched something in me. But we finally got over it. Anyway, we had a good chat that night at the party, and subsequently got on very well. Indeed a mutual respect grew between us, and we never talked about the incident again.

Later on, Pat became interested in the metaphysical, and joined the Rosicrucians. Nearly every day she would come to me and we'd discuss esoteric matters. I could see these talks were helping her tremendously, and that was the time we got as close as we were ever going to get. I used to enjoy those sessions, and they went on until the time she left.

Then she became involved in left-wing politics, which more or less pushed the interest in esotericism aside. And once Pat left she never seemed to find a vehicle for her considerable talents. But she had, as it were, outgrown the Street.

Her death from lung cancer was a bombshell. Pat always had a smoker's cough, it was almost a characteristic of hers. But it was a wretched end for someone so vital, so full of life, so *big*. Elsie Tanner was made by Pat, injecting her own personality into the character and having the writers pick up on it.

Her memorial service was remarkably moving. A jazz band played 'When the Saints Come Marching In', and everyone was laughing, even as the tears rolled down our faces. It was typical of Pat – brave and dramatic and flamboyant to the end.

One of the most popular and longest-running storylines

during Pat's time in the Street was her on-off romance with Len Fairclough. Peter Adamson was in his own way as powerful a personality as Pat, and like her, he made a significant contribution to fashioning the character he played.

His portrayal of the macho, yet essentially good-natured, Len was a very well-observed depiction of exactly the kind of working-class male one would expect to find in any real life Coronation Street. An intelligent and thoughtful man, Peter Adamson ran a repertory company in Bury before coming into the Street, and has written at least one play.

It's not telling tales out of school when I say he was an alcoholic. But he went to AA, got himself straightened out, and made it his mission in life to help others in the same situation. He did some splendid work in this regard.

He had a court case that was not pleasant. It was a tragedy to all concerned. I would not wish to go into the rights and wrongs of it, but the fact is he was acquitted. His leaving was a great loss to the Street, however, the idea that he left because of the case is incorrect. We are contractually obliged not to speak to the media without Granada's permission. Peter talked to the press without permission and was warned about it. He did it again and he was warned again. He did it a third time and was suspended. One of the very few suspensions there has ever been in the Street, I might add. And while he was suspended he did it again. That was the reason for him leaving.

Granada has always been a company that protects and looks after its people, and they behaved very well in this awkward situation. They were as tolerant and helpful as they possibly could be towards him. After the court case, they were ready to welcome him back. It was persistent breach of contract that in the end left them no choice.

Cecil and Sidney Bernstein ran Granada, and the company's supportive attitude towards its employees flowed directly from them. Both used to visit the studio regularly, and Sidney we held in particular awe. He knew everybody, down to the cleaners, and if he had a conversation with you he would remember it six months later. Even the technical guys said that when he stood behind them they were on tenterhooks because he knew as much about their jobs as they did.

I was late for work one day and didn't have time to shave, so I put an electric shaver in my pocket, with the intention of slipping off after the first scene and freshening up. I dashed in to Granada and flew through the lift doors with my shaver in my hand. The doors shut and there I was in the lift with Cecil and Sidney Bernstein. But being the great diplomats that they were, they started to discuss the pros and cons of various electric shavers.

Cecil Bernstein was a great friend and lover of the Street, and attended all our birthday parties. He was someone we could turn to and was always very helpful.

Arthur Lowe was in the Street from the first year, and he was a very private man. He had done a large and varied amount of acting work before he came into the Street to play Leonard Swindley. He was essentially quite shy and didn't like mixing outside work hours, or doing the personal appearances and so on that go with the Street. He wasn't easy to get to know, but I did get to know him. Anne Reid was very friendly with him, too. But other than that I don't think many people were.

I used to love watching him work because he was so meticulous and very amusing. He was superb in *Dad's Army*, and one of the main reasons why it became my favourite comedy show. A great deal of the humour he generated in that programme, and as Mr Swindley, came from this thing of trying to stand on his dignity in undignified situations. And his timing was immaculate. When he was delivering dialogue he would talk quite normally, then hit the Lancashire very hard on one word.

I liked Arthur and had enormous respect for his talents. But he wasn't someone who automatically or naturally became part of the team.

Now that repertory theatre is all but dead, series like *Coronation Street* have taken its place as seedbeds for new talent. Not just for actors, but writers, producers, directors and the whole panoply of creative people needed to keep a top-rating show on the screen. But of course the standard has to be high because everyone is so exposed at that level.

The number of actors who have gone through the Street, and in many cases subsequently built themselves careers in the public eye, is staggering. Some of the names that come to mind from the early days include Davy Jones, who went on to become a Monkee, of course, and Peter Noone, who also gained immense pop star status.

Joanna Lumley came in for a while as one of Ken's many girlfriends, and was very good to work with. I like to think the Street helped her on her way to things like *The Avengers*. She played the headmaster's daughter. Ken proposed to her and she rejected him. It was definitely his loss. Poor old Ken. Ever the loser.

We didn't quite know what we had during that initial thirteen-week run. But we all realised it was something very special.

I remember the first producer, Harry Latham, saying, 'What have we got here, Bill? What *is* this?'

The viewing figures grew very rapidly. *Coronation Street* first entered the charts in March of 1961, at number four, with 7.49 million households watching. By October it was number one. It has never been out of the top ten of the charts in the three decades since, usually occupying first or second place.

The opening episodes got some excellent reviews right across the range of the Press, from the tabloids of the day to *The Observer*, *The Times* and *The New Statesman*. Several of them referred to the Street's unique synthesis of drama, comedy and social documentary. Before the thirteen weeks were over, Granada offered us all three-year contracts.

We seemed to have hit upon some magic formula. It was hard to quantify exactly what it was, and to this day everyone involved has their own ideas as to why the Street continues to enjoy such popularity. I think it was because it was wholesome, earthy and set in a community that thrived and worked together. It showed that people cared. You got, and still get, a sense of well-being, and that human nature is basically good. It was a very moral sort of show. Plus, you're never far from a laugh; whatever tragedies are going on there's always a comedy element present. As in life.

Tony Warren, *Coronation Street*'s creator, turned in scripts with real depth, gritty reality and superb characterisations. Many writers came in after Tony, but the Street was his baby. He got it off the ground, established all the characters and set the pattern for his successors to follow.

It was only a couple of years ago, when I appeared with Tony on the television show *Good Morning*, that he first told me how I landed the part of Ken Barlow. As a character, Ken was a problem; an intellectual lad from a working-class street who was the first member of his family to attend university. (I often wondered whether the character was loosely based on Tony himself.) Apparently, while I was recording the play *Marking Time* at Granada, Tony saw me. He fetched the Street's casting director, Jose Scott pointed me out, and said, '*That* is Ken Barlow.' Obviously I had to have the initial interview and do the pilot, but Tony said that was the moment when they gelled it.

So I owe a lot to Tony Warren, as does the rest of the cast, Granada and, I venture to say, the Nation.

Tony's had a sort of on-off time over the years, but I'm delighted to say that his career as a novelist, with two well-received books published so far, is proving very successful. He is a highly creative, very personable chap, and if it wasn't for him there would have been no *Coronation Street*.

Many wonderful writers have worked on the show over the years. In the early days we had Jack Rosenthal, Geoffrey Lancashire (whose daughter Sarah is making such a success of Raquel) and Adele Rose – who is still with us – and we have always been so well served by them. The thing about the Street is that it's not story-based, it is character-based and so you can build a story around something like Mavis and her budgie and still hold the audience's interest. If a series is story-based, the stories have got to get stronger and stronger and more and more extreme, then you're really heading for trouble. So as long as a series remains character-based, love them or hate them, people know how they are going to react. I think that is the key. When you get a really strong story *and* strong characters, as is so often the case in the Street, you've got the greatest.

A system for generating the storylines was developed in the early days and, with a few refinements, it's still the one used now. We have a committee comprising the writers, the storyline editors and the producer of the day. They thrash out long-term storylines, for the following four or five weeks, say. This is initially done very broadly, deciding, for example, whether Ken will split with Deirdre, if Maggie will marry again, or Mike Baldwin will wed Alma. I gather these meetings are sometimes more dramatic than the show itself!

When the storylines are agreed and planned out the storyline editors go away and break them down into episodes. They then divide the episodes into scenes, producing a rough synopsis, and this is handed out to various writers. In any week there'll probably be two or three different writers at work – currently we have a pool of fourteen to draw on. If we had just one writer the plots would weave about all over the place; this system allows for continuity. The writers, having been involved throughout the creation of the storyline, then turn their attention to the dialogue. Good dialogue is the essence of a good script. And our writers are superb at this particular art. John Stevenson, Tom Elliott, Peter Whalley, Barry Hill and Julian Roach are among the more senior ones.

136

The cast don't quite know how the stories are going to go before we get our scripts. We may have a little bit of foreknowledge, but we're never quite sure *how* it's all going to happen. If you know you have a particularly tricky storyline coming up – an instance of this being when I knew Ken was going to have an affair with Wendy Crozier – you can get a little concerned. In that case, I was worried that as Ken had always been the good guy, the straight guy, whether the affair would play against his character. But in the event, it worked because it was so beautifully written and logically worked out.

The sign of a good storyline is when the viewers find themselves split between opposing characters. Once people start taking sides, you've got a strong story.

I gather some other drama series have writers responsible for particular groups of characters. I think that gets too inbred. If we did it in the Street, what would happen when everyone met in the Rovers, for instance? Our system ensures the writers are all involved in the overall creation and they stay fresh. Of course you find some writers relate more easily to certain characters, and some writers might have a slightly different idea of your character than you do, but it's up to the actor, working with the director, to reconcile such differences, which in any case are rare.

In common with all long-running shows, *Coronation Street* has what the industry calls a 'bible'. This list of stories and character traits is absolutely vital in order to avoid contradictions, inconsistencies and mistakes. Which the viewers would be the first to spot!

The Street's 'bible' was kept for years by a man called Eric Rosser, and Eric was very good. He retired not so long ago, and a remarkable young man called Daran Little took over the job. If you say to Daran, 'What was Ken doing in 1973?' or 'When's Ken's birthday?' he can tell you without referring to the mammoth volumes of records we keep. He is the walking *Coronation Street* 'bible'.

*   *   *

The producer is the person in charge of the whole team, and as such, occupies an incredibly important position. There have been twenty-eight producers in the life of *Coronation Street*. And they tend to stay for quite a while; Harry Kershaw and David Liddiment as executive producer had very long runs, and Bill Podmore was producer for thirteen years.

The producer is the one who decides who the writers are and which writers will have which scripts. The producer is also involved in casting and contracts, and has responsibility for the discipline and artistic content of the show. We've been blessed over the years with many good producers, and our present one, Carolyn Reynolds, is no exception. She has a particularly difficult task with the changing face of television, but is a caring and strong person.

But from 1963 to 1964 we had a producer called Margaret Morris and she decided a number of people had to be axed. I don't know whether she thought we were all getting too big for our boots or that change was necessary. I've never agreed with change for the sake of change. I agree that you have to accept it, in fact the only thing in life you can be sure of is change, but there must be a reason for it and it should be for something better. If it's not broken, don't try to mend it.

So we had our own Valentine's Day massacre. After a technical run-through we were brought into the green room and it was announced that a whole swathe of characters would be leaving, some soon, some later. This was a bolt from the blue. We'd all coasted along, enjoying ourselves and working hard. We were very happy.

Two cast members, Doreen Keogh and Ivan Beavis, left almost immediately. There was a great deal of unhappiness and discontent amongst the team. Then Margaret Morris left, and Harry Kershaw, the producer before her, came back in. I was in London at the time, and I remember him ringing me and saying, 'Forget all this business, Bill, we want everybody to stay'. He brought us back to the fold.

Harry Kershaw had always been the father of the Street in the sense that people would go to him. He was a warm, good man, and had the Street in his heart. He really steered the show, and acted as executive producer until 1972. Even when he retired he was always around and I'm quite sure he was consulted. He was one of the great producers of the Street.

I recall a humorous incident concerning Harry. There was a storyline in the seventies in which Norma Ford (Diana Davis) became besotted with Ken. She drooled after him but he didn't want to know. Norma asked Ken if he would give her private English lessons as a ruse to get him on his own in the evenings. He soon realised there was more to it than just the tuition and, being a sensitive chap he wanted to let her know there was no future in the relationship, but very gently. So he read a poem to her which started out as a love poem. The episode ended just as he recited the first couple of stanzas.

A young woman rang up the following day and spoke to Harry. 'That poem Ken read to Norma Ford is absolutely wonderful,' she enthused. 'Could you send me a copy? It's so romantic. I want to give it to my boyfriend.' Harry was terribly flattered. Because he'd tried to find a suitable poem he wanted, couldn't, and wrote it himself. So he got a copy, shoved it in an envelope and sent it off. When the next episode rolled around he remembered, to his horror, that this poem went on to say that love you though I do I'm afraid there's no future for us and it must end.

We don't know to this day what effect it had on the relationship between that girl and her boyfriend.

Directors tend to come and go more frequently. The schedule requires they work on a three-week turnover. In other words they will direct one week, edit the following week, and the week after prepare their script in readiness for the cycle to start over again. So typically, a director has two weeks off and one week working with the cast. This means we have three directors working in harness.

The director gives us our moves, directs us in performance, works out the shots and camera angles, and supervises recording. It's the director's job to emphasise what is dramatic. A good director you're not aware of; the show seems to whiz through and you get every little nuance of the story. The producer is around while this is all going on, of course, and frequently has an input.

In the first episodes the director was Derek Bennett – a brilliant man who used to *memorise* the scripts – and now well known for his morning programme *The Time, The Place*. Early producers were Mike Scott, Harry Latham, Derek Grainger and Dick Everett, who worked his way up from floor manager at Granada.

Derek Grainger, who produced us from 1961 to 1962, was the man who later produced *Brideshead Revisited*. When he was with us he talked about getting Marlon Brando to come over and appear in the Street. He had that sort of flair, and I loved it. Not that it happened, but it would have been wonderful. I'm a great admirer of Marlon Brando.

As with producers, we've been very lucky with directors over the years. But there has been the odd exception.

About twelve months into the Street we were working with a director, who shall be nameless, who had a drink problem. One week, he worked out his camera scripts and then disappeared. The floor manager and his PA took us through our lines and they gave the camera scripts to the chief cameraman. We all knew our characters well enough by then, and there was nothing particularly complex in the scripts, so it wasn't a great problem.

We got to the end of the week and dress rehearsals without sign of this director. After dress rehearsal, when we would all normally go to the committee room for director's notes, I saw him walking along the corridor towards me.

'Are you coming to give us notes?' I asked.

'No,' he said, 'you can give them the notes, Bill.'

'Oh, really?'

'Yes. You can just say you're a load of bloody amateurs.' And he marched off.

The cast was somewhat taken aback when I walked into the committee room and passed on the news that we were all bloody amateurs. Needless to say, that director didn't stay much longer.

But the lesson is that the Street was up and running; it had its own momentum by that time. Which is not to say a director isn't needed. It just so happened that particular one had done his initial work and we'd got away with it. A really good director lifts you up, improves your performance and puts everything together as a coherent whole.

Directors vary in the way they work with you, and obviously you work more easily with some, which is only natural. Apart from that one incident, the directors have always been of a very high calibre. I've never ever had a major problem with a director on the Street in thirty-two years. It's always been a good professional working relationship.

One I have a particularly soft spot for is Brian Mills. He did the Ken/Deirdre make-and-break scenes that hit the tabloids and got all the publicity. Brian is known for putting in all sorts of interesting shots – he'll have cameras hanging from the ceiling, as he did in the Ken and Deirdre sequences. The ceiling shot is a Brian Mills trademark.

I remember Anne Kirkbride and I preparing for the ultimate and most highly-charged scene in the Ken/Deirdre storyline. We worked very hard indeed to get the thing fundamentally right – getting the words and moves spot-on; getting everything sorted out technically. But we would hold back until the actual take and then – boom! – go for it.

We did a run-through beforehand. Then Brian came down and said, 'I think it could perhaps have a little *more*'. Both Anne and myself said together, 'We haven't done it yet, Brian.' 'Oh, great,' he said. He didn't need to say any more. So when we came to do it, it was fully-charged, and consequently the audience got more than their money's worth, I think. Brian is the ideal director; sensitive and extremely resourceful.

Floor managers have a vital function in a television studio – they are the director's spokesman on the set. Around 1965, Eddy Shah joined Granada as a floor manager, and we began a friendship that endures to this day. We used to play golf together; I got him in as a member of Prestwich Golf Club, I remember. Then he left and went his own way. But he lives not far from us, when he's not over in America now he's made his millions. Our family always goes to his house on Boxing Day and bonfire night.

He's doing very well as a novelist now – he writes bestselling thrillers – and pours out about 2,000 words a day. It's something he always wanted to do, but he made his money first with *Today* newspaper, of course.

Eddy is in the enviable position of being totally in command of his own destiny.

People often ask us how we physically put *Coronation Street* together. The schedule, like the writing process, was devised right at the start and, apart from some changes made when we went to three episodes a couple of years ago, remains basically the same.

At the beginning, Monday mornings were read-through time. This was when everybody learned what was in store for their characters. In the afternoon we moved to a rehearsal room where the floor was marked-out for positioning and a few tables and chairs were arranged around the place. This was so the director could give us our moves – you get up at this point, walk over there, come back here, pour yourself a cup of tea, sit down – that kind of thing. We went through that week's two episodes.

On Tuesday morning we rehearsed the first episode; in the afternoon we rehearsed the second. And you were expected to know them.

We had a rough run-through of both episodes on Wednesday morning. From two o'clock in the afternoon we had what we call technical run-through. This is, to many of us, the most frightening part of the week. Because that's when the producer, the writers, the cameramen, the sound men, the casting directors and various other people all come in to watch. It's the first time you have an audience. Technical run-through is a testing time. You get to know whether something's working or not.

All day Thursday was camera rehearsals. We were into the studio for the first time then and the sets were up. You slowly went through the script. You weren't really acting it at that stage, more talking through the lines. The camera moves and light and sound adjustments were finalised then.

Friday morning was the day you woke up knowing you had a live show at seven o'clock that evening and the nerves were starting to build. The day began with another run-through, followed by a full dress rehearsal after lunch. Then the whole cast went into a committee room to take director's notes, which meant going through the entire episode to identify its strengths and weaknesses.

As seven o'clock approached we all had to be in our sets waiting for the off. And in those days the studio was very small. I could sit in the Barlow's living room and reach out to touch the bar in the Rovers' Return.

The theme music swelled and we were on. The first scene took place and then the camera just literally swung over and you had to be sitting there ready, even if your scene might not be on until half-way through. The feeling of nerves was quite extraordinary.

So we did the show live, absolutely petrified, broke for an hour, then filmed the second episode between 9 and 9.30. That couldn't be edited. If something went wrong we had to go back to the top and do the whole thing again. Even then, we could do that only once.

There were some awful moments in the live days. I

remember dear old Margot Bryant drying up once. She just stood there and said, 'Oh dear,' and the camera cut off on to the next scene. But it was amazing what we got away with. I remember a scene where Ann Cunningham and Elsie Tanner were talking about a blouse in a shop window, and it wasn't there. Gradually you saw it sort of creep in. Live television, because it's a very technical medium, is, I think, too demanding. Unless it's a comedy show with an audience.

Anyway, after about three months, one of the technical unions had a strike, and the Street was held up. It put the whole schedule out of synch. From then on we recorded both episodes. It was in a way that still couldn't be edited, so it remained frightening. But not quite as frightening as totally live television.

That system carried on until colour came in, in 1969, when it began to get easier. The colour cameras would flood, the colours had to be rested and changed, so we started to have a slightly easier time with it. Although we continue to be nervous, it isn't *anything* like as terrifying as those early days.

What were we doing when we weren't in front of the cameras? Well, over the years, a number of fads and hobbies have occupied the cast during their rest periods. In the early days Vi Carson, Arthur Leslie and one or two others became obsessed with the *Telegraph* crossword. You always knew who finished first; he or she was the one who would start walking round the room and trying to get a peek at everybody else's. There was quite intense competition to see who could complete it first.

When Jean Alexander and Bernard Youens came in they instigated a Scrabble craze. Some of those games would go on for hours on end.

Then it was poker. Some of us started a poker school, and Alan Rothwell and I in particular began to take it very seriously. We bought books on the subject, studied it and worked really hard at improving our game. I used to have a little bag for my stake money, and if it wasn't up by the end of the week I could get really cross. I used to do all right because I worked at it. In fact I got to the point where I thought I was quite good at poker.

I knew there was a professional game of poker that went on at The Cabaret Club in Manchester every Saturday night. Alan and myself went and had a look at it on a couple of occasions. I decided I was going to get some money together and sit in. This was going to be the big test of my skills. I remember Gus Demmy coming up to us and saying, 'Don't go and sit in with that lot. Just watch.' But I was determined.

I got sixty pounds together – a tidy sum in 1961 – and sat in one night. There were six or seven people around the table. Four of them were chattering away. The other three were stony silent. As the night wore, on, the chatterers fell away and left me with the silent trio. Professional gamblers to a man. One of them wore a pinstripe suit and looked like a surgeon. He never said a *word*. We later found out he made a lot of money out of poker on a regular basis.

I was very nervous and sweaty-palmed, but did my best to play a tight game. They watch you, these guys, and if I hadn't got anything I stacked out. But you were always having to put a stake in, and if you keep doing that all night you're going to lose your money eventually. I got a good hand and decided to really push it. Immediately the three professionals stacked in. I made about a hundred pounds on that hand.

But by now they had the measure of me. In the early hours of the morning I got up from that table absolutely drenched to the skin, feeling as tense as anything and with sixty pounds in my hand – exactly what I'd sat down with. I was pleased about that, but the lesson I learnt was that I never wanted to play poker out of my depth again. In future I was going to keep it as a friendly game and only play with people of my own level. I knew I couldn't survive with people like the ones in The Cabaret Club that night.

There's a myth that actors must be good at poker because of the bluffing element. It isn't so. Poker is really about percentages; bluffing is very subtle and sparingly used. What you do is, you invest in your cards, remember what's gone, and know the likelihood of a certain card coming up. You've got to have a quick brain, a good memory and steely nerves. And the money mustn't be money, so to speak. Poker is money management, but if you're relating that to the bicycle you could have bought with it, don't bother.

Actors aren't good poker players generally because they invariably get too emotional. There's a great saying in the game: never try to bluff a bad player. Because he probably can't even see what you're doing.

Then the cast went on to bridge, which is a much more enjoyable game. The most fanatical players were Doris Speed, Bernard Youens, Brian Mosley and myself. I got very good at teaching people, quickly, how to play. It's a game that puts off a lot of people because at first sight it looks so complex.

Doris, if she got a good hand, would stand up; I don't know if she was worried that people were going to look at her hand. She really loved her bridge. When she left, the passion for the game cooled a great deal, and now it's long gone.

Apart from odd flurries of chess among one or two members of the cast, we don't have a main craze at the moment. Although in the summer some play croquet on the lawn in front of the studio. The busy new schedule does not give much time for collective games.

Nine

Because *Coronation Street* was such an immediate success, we were all thrown into the spotlight. Fame and recognition came overnight. People like Tom Jones and the Beatles came to Granada to meet us. Suddenly, we were big stuff.

Fame is a strange animal. There's no doubt about it, it makes you feel good initially. The recognition and attention is, I suspect, the reason most people become actors. Fame opens doors. People hail you in the streets. It gives you a lovely, warm, secure feeling. As a male, you begin to think you're a bit of a lad.

Then you move into a second phase, and in my case this came quite quickly. It begins to dawn on you that you can't switch this thing off. You can't go anywhere without being known. You can't have a clandestine meeting or spend a penny up a back alley without the Press getting on to it. Certain things are denied you, and anonymity is one of them. This can get a bit spooky. I remember going to the Orkneys, which is about as remote a part of the British Isles as you can find, to open a tea-room for my friend Selwyn Hughes. Within a few minutes of arriving, the whole village knew I was there. Going into the second phase isn't nice. You're seen by 'x' million people twice a week and even the ones who hate you, know you. You're trapped.

The third phase is the best and most important. This is

147

when you come to realise that fame doesn't make you any better or worse than anyone else. The analogy I use is that of a milkman. Everybody on his round knows him, it's part of the job. I just happen to have a pretty big milk round. It's simply a strange quirk of my job that people recognise me.

If you're lucky enough to make it to the third phase you start to get the perspective right. You understand fame doesn't mean anything other than that your face is well-known. You hope you're liked, of course, and that people enjoy your character, but you must get the balance right. Some actors who play the same character in a long-running series develop personality problems. I don't have a personality conflict because my character is fairly straight.

Ken Barlow has my mannerisms, my weight, my appearance, but what he says and does comes from the writers. I had to think about the Lancashire accent a bit in the early days, but because he's an educated guy, that slipped to being just a slight inflection, which I've probably picked up anyway. If I'd been playing somebody like Quasimodo for the past thirty-two years it might be a different story. But I know Bill Roache probably intruded more into Ken Barlow than Ken Barlow did into Bill Roache. I have no personality crisis.

I think fame is a privilege.

But it can also bring certain temptations and the opportunity to exploit them. As I found in the heady days of the 1960s.

I met the actress Anna Cropper when we were in rep together at Nottingham, and again later at Oldham. Shortly after *Coronation Street* started in 1961 we decided to marry. The marriage service took place at St John's Wood church in north London. Subsequently we had two children, Vanya and Linus.

We had a house outside Manchester and one in London, at 57 Colebrook Row, Islington, which runs parallel with Camden Passage. I had no idea how long *Coronation Street* was going to run, or how long I was going to be in it, so it seemed sensible to maintain a base in London. The family lived in Colebrook Row, and Monday to Friday I lived in the North, just getting home for weekends.

I don't think this is a particularly good basis for a marriage. But that is no excuse for my behaviour. Because, after a while, I led the life of a bachelor when I was in the North. I had the example of my parents, I had my own children, and I wanted a happy family life. But the sex drive is an extraordinary thing. Somebody once said that the day they got control of their sex drive, it was like being unchained from a lunatic. I can relate to that. But it's easy to say you have a powerful sex drive; it can be equally said you're weak in not controlling it. It's a struggle a lot of men have.

I wanted a good, wholesome family life. But I misbehaved. I had a lot of affairs with some very attractive and well-known women, and with some not so attractive and not so well-known women. But it wasn't the carefree bachelor life everyone envies. I always felt slightly tainted and guilty. So why did I do it? I don't know. I had no control over my urges, or my opportunities inasmuch as I was well-known. I did not behave well.

I'm not proud of what I did and have never boasted about it. I think the 'kiss and tell' syndrome is a form of prostitution and don't approve of it. I'm afraid there are those who like to read about this sort of thing; maybe it comforts them to see that other people are as normal and weak as they are. I believe in discretion in these matters, however, even if others have fed allegations to the media about me.

I'm not trying to whitewash things, but I don't want to go into the business of naming names about the women I had affairs with. I know a lot of people are going to be disappointed in reading this. But I think a moment of intimacy between a man and a woman, even if it's on only one or two occasions, is a very private moment, and not for the ears of others.

The sixties were an extraordinary decade, an era of liberation, and perhaps one is subject to the mood of the times. There was a great sense of freedom in the air in those days. But with freedom should come responsibility. I had the former but did not exercise the latter. And that is contrary to my nature. I like to think of myself as a responsible person, and yet my behaviour at that time was reckless and ultimately selfish.

I'm afraid this put a great strain on my marriage and we were eventually divorced.

I met my second wife, Sara Mottram, in 1972. Dick Everett, who was a floor manager at Granada when *Coronation Street* started, and became our producer in 1968, was responsible for us meeting. Dick lived in Wilmslow, and he and his wife were in The Green Room, the local amateur dramatics society. They were having a fund-raising evening for charity, to be based on the television programme *Going For a Song*, and needed a couple of personalities to take part. I didn't really want to do it. 'But if you can't get anybody else,' I said, 'let me know'. Which is always a fatal thing to say. Because, of course, he couldn't get anybody else and I was hooked in.

Sara, who was a model at that time, and also a member of The Green Room, had the job of bringing on the antiques we were supposed to identify. I found out later that she wasn't keen on being there either, funnily enough. But thank God, we both decided to go. Because I thought this slim, tall, elegant, dark-haired, blue-eyed woman was the most beautiful thing I'd ever seen. And I've never had cause to alter that opinion!

I know nothing about antiques whatsoever, but the evening was quite fascinating. Sara brought on a succession of bizarre looking objects and we had to work out what they were for. My team made some lucky guesses, and we won. I was awarded an antique ceramic plate, which still has pride of place in our home.

Sara and I bumped into each other during the interval and chatted briefly. She told me subsequently that as I walked away she said to herself, 'I'm going to marry that man.' Actually, it wasn't so much that she said it to herself, it more came to her. She just intuitively *knew* it was going to happen. At that point there was no similar thought in my mind. I was going through a divorce and re-marrying was the last thing I was thinking about. I just knew Sara was very attractive and very likeable. We met again at the party afterwards, and carried on meeting after that.

I won two prizes that evening.

We married four or five years later. It was a quiet registry office wedding; we didn't want any fuss or anybody to know. I'd taken the day off from *Coronation Street*, and the phone rang just as we were about to leave the house for the registry office. It was a colleague at Granada, and he said, 'You're supposed to be here at rehearsal, Bill.' 'No I'm not,' I said, 'I've got the producer's permission to be away today. I've got something important to do.' We kept it that quiet. When I asked Bill Podmore for the day off to get married he made a wonderful but cynical remark: he said 'Anyone who gets married for a second time doesn't deserve to have got rid of his first wife.'

Alan Rothwell was the best man, and Leita Donn, the *Coronation Street* press officer who looked after us like a mother hen, was there. Leita was a truly good person, a rare thing in the world of the press. We had the wedding breakfast at a restaurant called The Last Drop, which is a wonderful place up in the hills above Bolton.

They say a leopard cannot change its spots. But meeting and marrying Sara brought about a profound change in me. She transformed me into a man totally satisfied with married life. All my previous restlessness and romantic fecklessness completely disappeared. I knew it was possible to lead a wholesome family life and was so glad to be offered the opportunity to do so. It was, and is, a great relief. And my happiness was heightened all the more with the arrival of our children, Verity and William.

I'm proud to say that my daughter and son from my first marriage, Vanya and Linus, are making good careers for themselves in their respective professions. Vanya is working in the design industry. Linus had no other ambition than to act, and I'm pleased to say he's making a big name for himself.

He went to drama school and then on to the Royal Shakespeare Company at Stratford. After that, he was in a number of productions around the country, including an excellent version of *Love's Labours Lost* at the Exchange Theatre in Manchester.

Having got himself a good, classic foundation in acting, of the sort I wish I had gone for, he began to pick up some excellent roles on television. He has played Van Gogh and was the nasty detective in *Black and Blue*. As I write, Linus is appearing with Penelope Wilton and Nicholas Jones in Terence Rattigan's *The Deep Blue Sea* at the Apollo Theatre, Shaftesbury Avenue, which had great reviews. He is now well established and a much respected actor, which is a delight to me.

Ten

About a year into *Coronation Street*, and having the unaccustomed security of a three-year contract, I decided to buy somewhere to live.

I bought a little cottage, one of a row of three, in a place called Rawtenstall, in Rossendale. There had been an old mill nearby that had been pulled down, but the small mill chimney was still standing, and it was right next door to the cottage. I managed to buy this cottage, which was not much more than a two up, two down, *and* the mill chimney, for £400 freehold. I did it up, demolished the chimney and built a three-storey square tower in its place. I've always had a passion for towers. That became my first home and I lived there for six or seven years.

Then I heard that two cottages with nearly an acre of land attached were coming up for sale on the other side of Rawtenstall. A local builder told me the owner had died and they were going to be put on the market the next day. I found out who the estate agent was and, as he lived not far away, called on him that evening and handed over a deposit of one hundred pounds. The asking price was good and I didn't haggle about it.

These two cottages originally belonged to a big, Victorian mill owner's house nearby. One of them was habitable; the other was in a state of dereliction, with pigeons living in the rafters. But the real attraction was the acre of land at the front and the view of the rolling hills behind.

I renovated one cottage and sold the other to a local policeman. Then I built a bungalow on the land in front. I didn't employ an architect. I bought plans that came nearest to my specifications and found a builder to undertake the work. My intention was to site this bungalow myself. I'd look down into the field in front of the cottage every morning and decide where to drive the four huge wooden stakes I was using to mark out the ground plan. I must admit the positioning of these stakes was changed quite a lot because I couldn't make up my mind. This was partly because the ground had a gentle slope and partly because I was really determined to get it right.

I positioned the stakes one morning and went off to work thinking about *exactly* where I wanted the bungalow to be. When I got back that night the builders had dug the foundations. But as it happened it was absolutely spot-on.

We ended up with three fifths of an acre for a garden, and I planted it with some apple trees. The remaining cottage was sold off and Sara and I lived in the bungalow very happily for several years. Then she became pregnant and we needed more room. As luck would have it, we heard that the big mill owner's mansion, Sykeside House, was up for sale. We leapt at it. A beautiful place, with two-and-a-half acres of land, it was absolutely ideal.

At that time I was always trying to do things myself, and decided to do my own conveyancing. That was a mistake. Do-it-yourself conveyancing is fine so long as both houses are registered and there are no boundary or other problems. The first thing I discovered was that one of the houses was so old it hadn't been registered. Then a boundary problem revealed itself. Right in the middle of all this, the man buying my bungalow died. I was tearing my hair out. So I rushed to a solicitor who, fortunately, managed to sort out the mess.

Sykeside House was built out of big honey-coloured stone

blocks and stood three storeys high. It had a massive staircase sweeping up from the entrance hall with a large glazed window behind it. There were the most wonderful attics – I think they would have been servants' quarters in the old days – and I had them opened out to make a study.

The garden was old, with slightly decaying, overgrown paths and a huge lawn running along the side of one wall. There was a weeping ash in the front drive, rather like the one we had at Rutland House when I was a child. I always felt so relaxed and comfortable there. I really loved Sykeside House.

We eventually moved because Sara wanted to go back to her birthplace in Wilmslow, and because there were no schools nearby for our growing children. The people we eventually sold the house to completely renovated it and turned it into an hotel and country club. They built on a conservatory to accommodate what became one of the best restaurants in the area.

Our present house is next door to Sara's parents, Sid and Kay, and you can only get to us via a drive between our two properties. It's very private and not many people even know the house is here. Having Sara's parents so close to hand has been a real blessing. There's a gate connecting our gardens and the children can move from one house to the other without having to go out into the road. Verity and William both have rooms at Sid and Kay's, in fact, so they can stay there overnight if ever we need to go away. It's been a very useful arrangement.

Quite often having your in-laws living next door is not a good move, but in the case of Sid and Kay Mottram it's been terrific. They are the perfect in-laws.

Verity is a delightful, attractive girl, who has never been any trouble and is loved by everyone. William is a blue-eyed, fair-haired angelic looking boy – but he is a boy. When we meet people and William is either rolling on the floor or on the top of a cupboard they say, 'oh, you've got one of those.' Yes we have, but I would not change him for the world.

Eleven

The desire to appear in the theatre was still in my blood even after settling in to *Coronation Street*. But it was six years before I was able to do anything about it.

In August, 1967, the theatrical entrepreneur David Malcolm invited me to play the lead in a production of Richard Gordon's *Doctor in Love*, to be staged at Bradford's Alhambra Theatre. I must confess to some apprehension at taking it on. It was six or seven years since I last trod the boards and the old butterflies were stirring again. But the challenge appealed, and the money was good, so I decided to take the plunge.

I needed two weeks for rehearsal and one for the actual performance, but, fortuitously, the schedule meshed with some time off I was due from the Street.

The director was a man called Edgar Metcalf, freshly arrived from directing the Shakespearian Company in Australia. Paul Freeman, now a very well-known actor, was also in the cast. I must say it was almost traumatic going back to the stage after such a long hiatus. I had forgotten about the necessity to employ the correct breathing techniques to project properly, for example, and the sheer hugeness of the theatre as seen from the stage came as a shock. But all went well on the night and we had an extremely successful week.

I used to commute to the theatre from Rosssendale every morning and evening, despite it being quite a long and hilly drive. My routine was to have a drink or two in the bar following the show before setting out for home. But never too many; I've always been mindful of the need to keep a clear head when driving.

One night I broke this rule just slightly. I allowed myself three gins, which probably put me a little over the legal limit, but I felt fine. As I was driving home I realised the car was going to run out of petrol. It was about one o'clock in the morning and miles from anywhere so I was getting a little worried. Then I came to a steep hill that ran down towards a town called Bacup. At the bottom of this hill was a roundabout and a set of traffic lights. There was no other traffic around, everything was deathly quiet, so I switched off the engine and let the car freewheel down.

When I got to the bottom, the lights were red. As I could see there was nobody about, I screeched round the traffic island and through the lights, still with the engine off and on sheer momentum. Another hill came up and as I started to climb it, naturally I began to slow down. Just as I switched on the ignition again I saw the headlights of a car that seemed to come from nowhere. It pulled level with me and waved me over.

It was a police car, of course.

I thought, *Oh, no*. If ever I was caught in a horrendous situation, this was it. I got out and stood there as one of the two policeman came towards me shaking his head.

'I don't believe it,' he said. '*I just do not believe it*. You're breaking the speed limit, you tear round a traffic island nearly on two wheels and run a red light.'

Then he turned to his partner and called out, 'Come here. Take a look at this.' The other one ambled over and they both stared at me.

'Well, what have you got to say for yourself?' the first one asked.

I thought, *I'm finished*. I could see my licence going. And the publicity . . .

'I'm terribly sorry, Constable,' I mumbled. 'It's no excuse, but I was running out of petrol and – '

'You won't do it again, will you, Sir?'

'Er, no, of course not, I – '

'Because Ena wouldn't like it, would she?'

I hadn't realised they'd recognised me. 'No, Constable, she wouldn't,' I said, suppressing a smile of relief.

A small perk of fame, but it can sometimes work the other way, too.

The next play I did, about two years later, was John Bowen's *Disorderly Women*. It's a very strange one, a bit like a Greek tragedy. In fact it's about Dionysus, the Greek god of Chaos. I played a young king of a country whose women, including his mother, have all unaccountably gone up into the hills. The only way he can find out why is to go up there himself. But he has to disguise himself as a woman. When he finally gets there his identity is revealed and this screaming mob of females pulls his head off! I had to have a replica of my head made, with bits of flesh hanging off, to be held aloft.

This involved having a death-mask made. The man who was going to do it greeted me with, 'Don't worry, you'll be all right. We've taken out an insurance policy on you.' Very comforting.

He shoved straws up my nose and started slapping on the plaster. But I'm claustrophobic, and as he built up layer upon layer of plaster I just couldn't bear it. It was a complete nightmare. Eventually we had to stop and he ended up making the death-mask in two sections. I wanted to keep this replica head after the run was over, but somebody walked off with it.

We opened at a small theatre near Granada studios called The Stables. John Fraser played Dionysus, and John Bowen himself directed the production. I thought it would be wonderful to have the writer himself direct us, and he was very good, but when John gave us our first notes he said,

'I counted forty "er", "ums" and "whats" I did not put in the script. If I'd wanted them I would have written them.' So because he'd written it you had to get it absolutely spot-on. Mind you, he's a brilliant writer. It was a very strange play, but I enjoyed doing it.

Later, they decided to move it to the Hampstead Theatre Club, in Swiss Cottage, north London, and we ran there for three weeks to very good notices.

The next time I appeared in a play offered me the opportunity to pay back Oldham rep. I heard they were closing for refurbishment for quite a few months, and they were worried sick about restarting, so I offered to put on a production to open the new season. They readily accepted.

I put together a production of that wonderful black farce *Arsenic and Old Lace*, and persuaded Jean Alexander to play one of the homicidal old dears. It was the only play she was ever enticed to do. Bernard Youens was the mad uncle, Brian Mosley was a policeman, and I played the lead. We ran it for three weeks, to full houses, and it started the theatre off again very satisfactorily I think.

The tragedy nowadays is that you cannot put on big cast plays for financial reasons. *Arsenic and Old Lace* has a cast of about seventeen and not all of them can be doubled-up.

I always wanted to form a film company. I've never had the desire to direct, but would love to have acted in films and produced them. In fact one subject I would still love to bring to the screen is the life of Sir Richard Burton, the Victorian explorer who discovered the source of the Nile, and translated *The Perfumed Garden* into English. He led an absolutely incredible life. I've read books on him and have even done some work on a screenplay. I went to see his extraordinary tomb at Mortlake – built in the shape of an Arabian tent – and his home in Camberwell. He was a fascinating character.

However, as Sara had done some acting, and I wanted to

try my hand at producing plays, we did decide to establish our own theatrical company, William Roache Productions. The manager of The Charter Theatre, at the Guildhall in Preston, Vin Sumner, wanted to encourage live theatre there and he was very helpful.

We produced four plays at Preston, but I didn't leave *Coronation Street* to work on them. I did the Street during the day and performed in the evenings. I'll never do that again. It was incredibly punishing.

Our first play there was *Blithe Spirit*, by Noel Coward, and it went very well. I played the lead and Sara was the wife – the non-ghostly one. We had an excellent director called Diana Harker, and I was very happy about that first production. It was beautifully staged.

I was a little nervous; it was my own company and I was the leading man, after all, and I had the usual opening night jitters. The curtain went up, the play started, and very early on my character has to make some drinks. As I came forward to hand them over my hand was shaking violently. It was as if the whole thing of running the company, and playing the lead, coupled with nervousness, manifested themselves in my hand. Anyway, I got over that.

The next one we did was Andre Roussin's sophisticated comedy *The Little Hut*, which was filmed in the fifties with Stewart Grainger, David Niven and Ava Gardner. It's about three people, Henry, Philip and his wife, who find themselves shipwrecked on a desert island. In evening dress! Henry is the wife's lover, and the comedy centres around them agreeing to a *ménage à trois*. The man who isn't with the woman has to sleep in the hut. Eventually a red indian appears, who turns out to be the Swedish cook from the ship. There's also a monkey at the end, which was a child actor in a skin. Diana Harker again directed.

We had six tons of sand delivered to the theatre to give the full desert island effect. Years later, they told me, they were still trying to get rid of it.

Sara was the woman and I was her husband. Brian Mosley, who plays Alf Roberts in *Coronation Street* and has a real flair for comedy, was the other man. Another actor called Laurence Mullen, who was also in the Street at the time, played the cook.

Oddly enough, although the play has a very English feel about it, it is in fact a translation from the French. It's such a funny play, but also a very tricky one. When we started to play it we found some difficulty in getting the style right, and during the first week of rehearsal I thought, this is going to be disastrous. But as we entered the second week we began to get into the flow of the play and the characterisations.

There's a scene where this red indian/Swedish cook is tied to the ship's mast and he's ranting and raving. Brian Mosley, whose character was a very friendly, bumbling sort of fellow, had to walk towards me and say, 'My God, this chap's going berserk. We can't have any of that.' Very sort of English, as I say, and in itself not particularly funny. But it was a trigger to me.

The dreaded giggles struck.

I got a bit helpless. 'We'll go back over that bit,' the director said. Brian did it and I was off again. It just welled up and I giggled and giggled.

'Okay, come on, let's get this done properly,' Diana said, a little more sternly.

This time I exploded before Brian had a chance to say anything.

'Obviously Bill's getting a bit of a thing here,' Diana remarked with incredible understatement. 'I want you all to help him by turning away. Don't look at him.'

That just sent me into absolute paroxysms of giggles and I was by now quite helpless.

The director was beginning to get a bit cross. 'Now look,' she said, 'this is no good, we're not getting anywhere here at all. I'm going to come up on stage and stand by Bill and we're going to do this *properly*.'

So she came and stood by me, Brian opened his mouth and she collapsed. We rolled about. We choked. Tears ran down our cheeks.

I was saved when, just as I was getting myself together, Lawrence Mullen pulled a face. He tried to make me laugh. That turned me to ice. I wasn't having that. No way was I going to be *made* to giggle, that did it.

At one point I honestly thought I'd have to give up acting because I had no control over this giggling. There are times in *Coronation Street* when I really have to fight the urge. The other great giggler in the cast, incidently, is Eileen Derbyshire – Emily Bishop. If we have a serious scene together, and we see that twinkle in each other's eye, it's awful. You know you've got to get it over and get out before it starts. Because once a giggle starts it becomes built-in and you've had it.

If it's deeply in, you've just got to turn away and try to think about something serious. You've got to concentrate very hard and say to yourself, okay, it's funny, let's accept that and get on with it. Olivier was a giggler; a lot of well-known actors have been gigglers. So at least I'm in good company.

William Roache Productions produced two more comedies at Preston after *The Little Hut*. We did *Flip Side*, with Timothy Carlton, Diane Mather and Peter Alexander, who later became very well-known in *Emmerdale Farm*. The last one was Alan Ayckbourn's *Time and Time Again*, featuring John Forgeham, Roy Holder and my wife Sara. Diana Harker took a rest for that one and Brian Mosley directed.

All these plays were successful and we never did less than break-even with any of them. Considering we had no subsidy and were a new company in a theatre which had no regular audiences, that was pretty good. But the *work* and the *time* – we were absolutely shattered by the end of it. I only appeared in *Blithe Spirit* and *The Little Hut* but trying to double-up with *Coronation Street* was still almost too much. On any kind of a regular basis it would have been impossible. But we did it.

I must say that working on the other side of the fence and experiencing the problems management faces was a real eye-opener. It was very interesting to have to look at things like budgets. Whereas actors moan about this, that and the other, when you suddenly find yourself having to make ends meet, you gain a much greater understanding of what's possible. The simplicity of just having to concentrate on your own acting was wonderful after doing that.

Mind you, having to audition other actors was something I hated; I wanted to give everybody the part. And a funny thing is, that people who do well at auditions are not necessarily the best ones for the job. You really do need to go and see them at work if you can. Some people are very confident and reassuring, and read very well, yet when it comes to actual playing, they're not as sensitive. On the other hand a truly sensitive, possibly superb, actor may not do that well at auditions.

Acting is an ensemble thing. It's like music – the words have to flow in harmony and the timing is vital. You get some actors who are very selfish. They will tread on your lines, deliberately cut in, upstage you and be generally uncooperative. You don't discover anything about that sort of thing until you're actually operating. So often it's far better to have people you know because you've already worked with them.

After the plays William Roache productions produced two Sunday night chat shows and Gordon Burns introduced them. At the first one we had Cliff Richard, which was a sell-out of course, and he was delightful, as was his manager Bill Latham. The second one had Frankie Vaughan as the guest. Cliff was a great fan of the *Street* and said he had been on a diet since Minnie Caldwell had called him 'The chubby little chap' in one episode.

What we really wanted to do after Preston was get a production together and tour with it. Circumstances conspired against us and it didn't happen, but we gave a lot of thought to taking out *A Man For All Seasons*. We considered a lot of names for the cast. I would have liked Roger Moore as the lead. And for the part of The Common Man, a sort of Everyman character who steps forward to talk to the audience and introduces sections of the play, I would have loved Les Dawson. He would have been absolutely brilliant at that. Les's death was a shock and I shall miss him. I had known him well over the years and played in his golf tournament. Once, when I was visiting his home, his little girl asked mine, 'What is it like having a famous daddy?'

Although the theatre is essential for learning the craft of acting, and a live audience is stimulating and exciting, I have no desire to go back. I prefer the intimacy and honesty of the small screen. It is much easier to just 'be'. Maybe this is my laziness again.

Twelve

One consistent interest throughout my life has been sport. At school I was in the first fifteen rugby team – playing scrum-half and wing-forward – and just about got into the cricket first eleven.

I also played a game known as fives. This takes place in a contained court with a kind of stone buttress at one end, called a pepper box, which you have to hit the ball into. In the old days it was played against the church wall. It was a hardball game, and you hit the ball with your hand, wearing a padded 'fives' glove. But most of us found that, after our hands went through a semi-swollen stage, they would become very tough and we didn't need the glove.

Shortly after *Coronation Street* started I discovered that the local YMCA, just up the road from Granada, had a fives court. I remember feeling a little embarrassed when I joined, because on the application form it said, 'Reasons for joining', and I wrote, 'Use of sporting facilities'. I thought I'd be thrown out, but they didn't seem to mind. I played fives for a while there, but as no one else I knew played, it fell away.

It's an exhilarating game and I'm surprised it isn't more widely known.

I played a bit of rugby in the Army, and a tremendous amount of cricket in Jamaica – what I could remember of it before the rum started flowing – and it was out there that I took up squash. The thing I like about squash is that you can play any hour of the day or night; bad weather and poor light have no bearing on it because it's an indoor sport. You never have far to go to pick the ball up and you get intense exercise in a short time. I grew quite fond of squash. I wasn't brilliant at it, but I could play well enough to enjoy it.

It was Bernard Youens who said, 'Why don't you try golf?' I was approaching my forties by this time and games like rugger and cricket were getting a bit hard. But I was a little reluctant to consider golf. I had always thought of it as a game for old men. My mother and father had been great golfers – my mother was a twelve handicap golfer – and we had silver spoons and cups which they'd won all over the house. They played right up to the war, but never took it up again afterwards. I'd hacked around a bit with a golf club but regarded it as a game I wouldn't want to play until I was virtually decrepit.

But Bernard, who was universally known as 'Bunny' by the way, presented me with a *fait accompli*. We used to get Thursday mornings off in those days, and one Monday he said, 'I've fixed you a lesson at Prestwich at eleven o'clock this Thursday morning'. Prestwich Golf Club is quite a small course, just north of Manchester, and as it was only a fifteen-minute drive I thought I'd give it a go.

So I went along and had this lesson with a delightful pro called Dave Wills. Dave was nice. He let you go and then worked on you. I hit two balls really well and remember thinking, I had a couple of good shots there. I've just got to do that all the time. I bought some clubs, started to play on a regular basis and was hooked in no time. As soon as I realised what a complicated and skilful game it was I became a total fanatic. I read all the books, worked hard, and took it very seriously indeed.

I wouldn't even allow myself on a golf course until I'd got reasonably competent. Because there's a tremendous

166

etiquette; people don't like you messing around or being slow and there are all sorts of rules. So I had lessons, learnt theory and enlisted people to help me. When I got to the point where I had a head full of theory and hours of practice behind me I decided I wanted to go out. But on my own. I desperately didn't want anyone around to distract me. Or to comment on my level of expertise, to be honest.

I got myself on to the first tee at Prestwich very early one morning when there was nobody about. Whenever I'd hit a golf ball before there had always been someone around telling me what to do.

Did I say there was nobody around? Correction. The green keeper was there. He stopped working, as they do if somebody's about to hit the ball, and just as I was lining-up he came over and said, 'Do you mind if I . . .?' and proceeded to instruct me. I could have wept. But golf, I've discovered, is a game where people *love* telling you what to do.

As the months passed, my passion remained undimmed and I worked and worked on the game. I was part of a regular Thursday-morning four with Bunny, Graham Habberfield and Eddy Shah. Alan Browning, who married Pat Phoenix, was there occasionally too.

But come eleven o'clock Bunny and Graham wanted to be off to the bar and get the drinks going. I was just really enthusiastic about the golf. Before long I had a reputation for going out whatever the weather. I played in snow and high winds; I even played in the dark one night. I was so dedicated to it. But my golf never got anywhere because the people I played with weren't really all that keen.

Then someone asked me to join the Variety Club Golf Society, and I went to one of their tournaments, where you play with professionals. There would be a celebrity, a professional and two amateurs, who bought in, which was how they raised money for charity. Consequently Gordon Brand was the first pro golfer I played with, and I began to see what *real* golf was like. My game improved immediately.

The Variety Club tournaments are wonderful. You play during the day and there's a dinner in the evening. These dinners are probably the best cabaret you could have anywhere. Not that anyone could afford the line-up of talent present. I got to know Frank Carson, Jimmy Tarbuck, Bruce Forsyth, Eddie Large, Tom O'Connor, Eric Sykes, Harry Secombe, – and a lot of them have their own golf tournaments. And once they know you're on the circuit, you get invited to them; I've played in the Harry Secombe, the Eddie Large, the Terry Wogan and many others. The whole year, just about every Sunday, you can be in one of these matches. Always raising money for charity, always playing really nice golf, and with a wonderful evening's entertainment to top the day. I grew to enjoy them enormously.

In due course I became a member of Prestwich Golf Club and began to play a serious, competitive game. Meanwhile, Bunny, Graham and the rest had all sort of fallen away and I was left on my own. I moved in with serious golfers at that point and almost immediately my handicap fell. On the way home from Granada I'd stop off at the course and play. It might only be one hole, it might be three holes, it might be eighteen holes in the summer, but nearly every day I'd play and my handicap went down to eleven.

I was absolutely thrilled to be asked to play in the last Bob Hope tournament at Rickmansworth Golf Club. You partner some wonderful professional golfers there; I played with Mark McNulty, and Gordon Brand again, amongst others. And the Bob Hope draws enormous crowds. You get on to the first tee there and find yourself facing a horseshoe of about 350 people. Everyone is introduced to the crowd before they tee off – the two pros and then the personalities.

I always do well when there's an audience, and that first hole in the Bob Hope was a par four. I got a par on it every time, and the same coming back at the eighteenth. Most people are terrified of being watched when they play. Not me. Perhaps it's the ham actor in me, but when people are watching my concentration's better. I have a philosophy. I think, if I miss this they're all going to love me anyway, because they like to see you vulnerable. The celebrities aren't really there because of their golf, that's what the pros are for, none the less I usually do well when there's somebody watching. It was a good four days, the Bob Hope, and at the end there was a big cabaret starring Bob himself.

One amusing thing happened during the Bob Hope, which took place just before a Ryder Cup tournament. I was on the practice area, in line with Sandy Lyle and several other top pros, when Bob Hope came up, said hello and shook hands with me. He watched me hit a couple of shots and then said, 'Are you playing in the Ryder Cup?' I thought, if only, if only! He was obviously very impressed with my swing. I had a photograph taken with him and it's a treasured possession.

Another big celebrity tournament is the Howard Keel, held every September near Knutsford. Two years ago I partnered with Eddy Shah and we won it. Jack Lemmon came over on that occasion, and in the evening I found myself singing on stage with him, Howard Keel and a host of British celebrities.

Howard is the most charming and sensitive man. He's another one of those people like Olivier; he's got immense kindness and is so totally unassuming. And he is an extremely good-looking and elegant chap to boot. Willy Morgan, the footballer, has a company which organises the event and it's become one of the best pro-celebrity gatherings in the country. I really get my golf going for that one.

I've also been asked to play three times in the televised pro-celebrity golf competitions. The first time was in 1982, at Turnberry, where I played with Johnny Miller against Nick Faldo and Gareth Edwards, the Welsh scrum-half. Sean Connery was one of the competitors, I remember. I was very, very nervous; Terry Wogan and other keen players who go up for this one say it's the most nerve-wracking. I think this is because the tournament is filmed and you know your game is going to be immortalised. It really is quite frightening.

The weather wasn't too good that year. And Nick Faldo, although a little reserved, probably because he was just starting out, was very pleasant. But I have to say that, although all the golf professionals I've met have been absolutely delightful, the sole exception was Johnny Miller. He wasn't helpful at all and he took no notice of me as his partner.

On one hole I'd done a lovely little chip out to very near the pin, and as I walked up on to the green he snapped, 'Don't walk on the line of the putt!' Later on I had a very long putt to do which was quite tricky and I asked if he would help me read it. He said, 'Ask my caddy.' Everybody stayed at the same hotel at Turnberry and we all had dinner together in the evenings. All but Johnny Miller. He stayed somewhere else, surrounded by his entourage, totally separate from the rest of us. He has been my only unpleasant experience in golf.

In 1987, again at Turnberry, I partnered Gary Player against Tony Jacklin and Terry Wogan. That was one of the most memorable matches I've taken part in. Gary Player is the most delightful of all men. He has a reputation for being very serious, but that's only because he takes his game so seriously. Even now, in his fifties, he looks as if he's only just discovered the game. He's terribly enthusiastic, and he works with you and is thrilled to bits if you hit a good shot. He's forever encouraging and instructing you. I absorbed every word he said and loved playing with this golfing legend.

I was in a bunker at one point, and Gary's known to be one of the world's greatest bunker players. He gave me some instructions on how to play this shot and the ball floated out and landed about a foot from the pin. I thought, if only he could be with me every time time I have a bunker shot!

You only play nine holes in television pro-celebrity. We were one down as we went on to the green at the eighth. I had a putt first to win, of about four foot, and took ages over it. I knew if I got that putt, and we won the hole, we'd go into the ninth all-square, and with a chance. I took my time and waited until I felt relaxed. I putted it and it went in. To be able to help someone like Gary Player, because of course the handicap system makes that possible, was just wonderful. So we went to the last hole level pegging. Again, I had a putt to win it, and I did. The whole thing was a thrill, mainly because of Gary Player. When he got back to his home in Cleveland, Ohio, he wrote me a letter saying how much he had enjoyed playing with me. A typical kindness from a very generous man.

I played with him again at a four-day tournament in November, 1991, at Dromoland Castle in south-west Ireland. We were up against Sandy Lyle and Craig Chalmers, the Scottish rugby fly-half.

Gary was as helpful as ever and, knowing his reputation for superb putting, I asked him what the secret was. 'Well,' he said, 'you know that in golf you have to keep your head still? When you putt you've got to keep it *absolutely* still.' I tried this and it made an incredible difference. Now when I'm putting I keep my head completely still because a slight sway makes the whole impetus go.

Again, we had a situation where we were all equal on the eighth. The ninth was a ghastly little hole where the fairway narrowed to a point with a tree in it, and it was hard to see how to get your ball through. There were woods on one side, a river on the other. Believe it or not, Gary Player hit into the woods. And these were really deep, thick woods. He had two goes and couldn't get out. I couldn't believe it. There was I, having to play against Sandy Lyle and Craig Chalmers to win the hole.

Gary came up and said, 'What are you going to do here, Bill?'

'I'm going to take a five wood and try to blast through.'

'No,' he said, 'take an iron.'

I followed his advice and got a shot that landed just on the edge of the green, about thirty-five feet from the pin.

When we got up on the green I knew that if we could get down in two putts we were going to win because our opponents had putted out. But thirty-five feet is a lot of putting. Gary said, 'Go on, do your practice swing. Let me see how you're going to hit this ball.'

I did.

'No,' he said, 'you've got to follow through much more than that,' and he lay down on the ground by my ball. 'Go on,' he said, 'do your thing,' and he put his hand where he wanted my putter to finish.

I swung again.

'Yes,' he beamed, 'follow through to there.'

If I follow through to there it's going to go right through the green, I thought. But I did exactly as he said and the ball landed four feet from the pin. He got up and said, 'Well, Bill, it's up to you. Go straight for it.'

The parallels with that previous match were uncanny. But I took my time, got it, and we won. Gary was thrilled to bits.

I've also played with Bernhard Langer at Fulford, in Yorkshire, where the Benson & Hedges golf tournament used to be. It's now moved down to the South and I can't get there any more. Three episodes of *Coronation Street* a week and working on Sundays has stopped me playing a lot of these games. But when it was in Fulford I played with Bernhard Langer and Sandy Lyle there. Bernhard Langer was wonderful; he held up the whole game at one stage to give me a lesson on the tee about locking my right hip and riding up on it.

At one hole I hit the ball into the trees. I went over and there were four spectators standing around it saying, 'You'll have to chip out sideways on to the fairway.' They'd worked it all out. But I don't like that sort of advice; I prefer to have a go. I looked towards the green and saw there was a hole in the leaves of the tree inbetween. It was only three or four feet wide. But I thought if I could work out the right trajectory and get the ball through that hole it might land on the green.

Bernhard Langer came over and asked what I was going to do. I told him I was thinking of having a go at getting through that hole. 'Yes,' he said, 'go on.' My little crowd of backseat players – these four spectators – voiced their scepticism. I ignored them, took out my pitching wedge and concentrated. When I hit that ball it floated through the hole and landed only a few feet from the pin. And those men followed me around for the rest of the game absolutely awe-struck. It was one of these incredible shots you probably couldn't do nine times out of ten. But every so often in golf you can hit a shot worthy of the best professionals. The thing about the pros is, they hit them more often.

I forget that my face is known and just tend to go about my life as a normal guy. Once, when I was at an Eric Sykes golf tournament, John Jacobs, who was the great teacher of the game and an absolute hero to me, held a clinic. He was going to make himself available to talk to any of us who were playing for half an hour before the match. This was too good a chance to miss and I determined to meet him. But I was held up and arrived just as he was due to finish.

Everyone but my idol had gone and he was packing away his clubs. I dashed over to him and he looked up, grinned broadly, and exclaimed, 'Oh! I must tell you how much I enjoy *Coronation Street*'. I couldn't believe it and blurted out, 'Forget all that! I've always wanted to meet you. Can you just tell me . . .?' And he gave me a little private tuition. He said, 'It all starts with the grip. Get your grip right, get your hands right, and everything else follows.' It was lovely. And it was so nice that he liked *Coronation Street*.

I started my own golf classic in 1991, raising money for the East Cheshire Hospice, of which I am vice president. Willy Morgan's company organised the event. The problem is that you have to find a sponsor. I was lucky enough to meet a delightful businessman Robin Arnold, and he sponsored my first golf competition, which raised 6,000 for the Hospice. We did the same again the second year.

Unfortunately, this year, because of the recession, it doesn't look as though we will be able to mount the tournament. Everyone has been hit in the current economic climate. But we'll be back.

Robin Arnold has become a close friend and we have a weekly tennis game at Match Point. I always think that he is too nice to be a businessman.

Playing golf teaches you a lot about people. It teaches you a lot about yourself. Golf forces you to harmonise your body, mind and emotions, almost like a sort of meditation. In fact, I would say without question that when I later started meditating my golf improved.

Golf is all rhythm. The club swings through, the body has to turn, the weight has to shift; it's a balletic movement of your whole body and being, in harmony. Your ankle joints, knee joints, hip joints, backbone, neck, shoulders, arms, wrists – if any one of them is half an inch off-line you're going to mis-hit the ball. And hitting it hard and a long way, possibly 250 yards or more, is not easy.

It's a very, very difficult but wonderfully exhilarating game when you get it right. When it's a lovely day out there on a parkland course, and you're striking the ball, well, it's the most beautiful feeling in the world. I shall always play golf while I am able.

About three years ago Ian Wilson, a solicitor friend of mine whose daughter goes to the same school as Verity, asked if I would play in a celebrity tennis tournament. Ian and his wife Ruth have become good friends of mine and Ian has been very helpful and comforting in difficult times. This was to take place at a local club called Match Point. He said Cliff Richard and some professional tennis players were coming up for it. 'But I don't play tennis,' I protested. 'That doesn't matter,' he said. 'You can come on as a sort of turn.'

But my philosophy is that if I do anything, I like to do it well. Being naturally quite a good sportsman, and having played a bit of tennis as a young lad, I asked Ian to give me a lesson. I started going along to Match Point regularly and ended up playing in that tournament. I did okay, although I had to get a few laughs to cover my fairly inadequate playing! On meeting Cliff again he said, 'I didn't know you played tennis, Bill.' I told him I'd only just started.

'I have my annual tennis tournament in Brighton,' Cliff said, 'and we get some very interesting people. Virginia Wade will be there and Des O'Connor has promised to come along. Would you like to be there too?' I said I'd love to.

So that December I went down to Brighton and stayed at the Grand Hotel. The tournament was held at the enormous conference centre next door and I'd got my tennis going by then. The high point for me was playing the marvellous Virginia Wade. And I played one match against Jo Durie, who was smashing. Des O'Connor, who had flown in from Florida specially, and Alvin Stardust added to the tremendous sense of fun.

Cliff Richard himself is a superb player, almost up to professional standard. He plays every day and is quite frighteningly good; he's not just a guy who likes tennis, he's totally dedicated to it. Amanda Barrie also played in that tournament, and Ken and Alma were just begining to have their affair. We were wired with radio mikes and there was patter going on throughout the games.

So I added tennis to the rota of pastimes to get obsessive about. And four years ago I found another.

My daughter, Verity, wanted to ride. She went on and on about it, so we took her along to the local riding school and she had some lessons. Now, I've never been a spectator, and I thought as I was at this riding school I'd give it a spin. My sister had a pony when we were young, but I was more interested in my bike. I did go to a residential riding school in the summer holidays at Rydal a couple of times, but I'd never thought seriously about pursuing it as a sport.

So there at Verity's riding stables I found myself joining in.

Before I knew what was happening, they were popping me over jumps. We bought Verity a pony. Then I needed a horse, so we got a horse. After that Verity needed another pony, because she started doing really well and was displaying a natural aptitude. She's not just a little girl with a hobby – she's qualifying at a very high standard and has a room full of rosettes. We've now reached the point where she's got three ponies; in fact we've got six horses all together.

My riding came along in – if you'll excuse the expression – leaps and bounds. I'll never forget the day I found myself on a seventeen-hand horse hurtling over a four-foot jump. You're really think you're on Pegasus and need an oxygen mask. You're looking between the ears of this massive beast and thinking, 'What am I doing? It's really quite frightening. But it's also incredibly stimulating.

We go to shows every weekend in our horse box, which often means being up at five o'clock on Saturday and Sunday mornings. Sara is absolutely wonderful at all the organisation. She used to ride herself, but whip-lashed her neck, so she's the one who gets all the tack ready and does the organising.

We have our own instructor called Paul Hughes who manages the yard. Paul is a great rider and teacher, but above all he's got a real rapport with horses. People come to the stables with horses that have problems and he soothes them down and sorts them out. The last member of our little team is Wendy, who is also a highly competent instructor and rider.

We're getting quite formidable now, and the riding has become a very serious activity. William has got his own pony and is just having fun with it, but has already won a rosette. Verity is a consistent winner and rarely comes home unplaced. This year she has competed at country level with the British Show Pony Society. She is showing a keen interest in dressage. One of her ponies, Ashlands Candyman, has recently been affiliated to the BHS dressage group. But her first pony Frankie will always be her first love. We also have a two-year old, Jasper, who has qualified for the Royal Show at Hickstead.

At the moment we have our horses at a place called Mottram St Andrews, in the Wilmslow Old Road Stables, owned by Mary and Stanley Dawson, who used to have a riding school. I'm very fond of Mary and Stanley and in the summer we have wonderful barbecues in their garden. Stanley is the kind of man who can turn his hand to anything and is a great comfort to have around. But at some point we'd like to move house and get a place with our own land for the horses. I want about twenty acres if possible, a few stables and a nice house, so we can all enjoy country life. I think that's an ideal worth working towards.

Bill Waddington has successfully bred racehorses for many years and we shared one with him called Let's go, Sabo. To our great excitement it won first time out, but never did anything after that. We now stay with what we know.

Thirteen

I have made some reference to my interest in the esoteric and mystical. In retrospect I can see this interest goes back a long way, and it now seems it was almost inevitable that I would come to search more deeply into these matters.

In my early family life, as I mentioned, there were stories about my grandfather, William Hugh Roache. His fascination with hypnotism and alternative medicine, his Freemasonry and adherence to theosophy – his open-minded approach to all things hidden and mysterious – was not shared by my father. But it's curious how a particular predilection, skill or talent will often skip a generation, and this seems to have happened in my case.

My two years at Michael House, the Steiner school grandfather helped to establish, must have sown some seeds. Steiner's ideology was predicated on bringing out the artistic and spiritual side of the human psyche through creative endeavour. This mainly took the form of music and movement; the curriculum contained no overt religious teaching. But a spiritual ethos was always implicit. Had I stayed there longer than I did, perhaps my path to spiritual awakening would not have been so prolonged.

It could have been because my father was a doctor, with illness and dissolution a daily fact of my childhood, but as a youngster I had a terrible fear of death. To the extent that I couldn't even bear to hear the word. Death seemed so final, so awful. Being a somewhat shy, introverted boy I couldn't express this terror, and it stayed with me as I matured into adolescence.

By that time my curiosity about the metaphysical had opened out. I wanted to know, if there was a God, why He didn't reveal Himself. Why did this God I was told existed allow wars, disease, cruelty, torture, loneliness and the thousands of other agonies that plagued human existence? Why should some people be born into poverty-stricken deprivation and others into a life of luxury? What happened after death? What was I to make of this story about Armageddon, when the last trumpet would sound and we were all supposed to rise from the dead? What state were we going to be in? What about those who died in infancy, did they remain infants for eternity? It all seemed a terrible mess. Yet somewhere within me I felt there were answers to these questions.

But when I put them to the people I felt could provide the answers – my headmaster and the chaplain at Rydal School, for example – I was told 'Well, God works in mysterious ways,' or, 'It's better you don't know about that.' I felt as though I was just being fobbed off.

I also had what I can only describe as a preoccupation with infinity. I would look at the night sky, see the stars, and wonder what was beyond them. And beyond *that*. If you could send out a spaceship that generated its own fuel, where would it end up? I went through awe, to fear, to absolute panic when I thought about this, and actually reached a stage where I couldn't look up at the sky. The stars were too meaningful, too frightening. I felt vulnerable sitting on this tiny little planet floating around in space.

I got cross that I couldn't get answers from anyone about all this, and became a sort of agnostic. But even then I remember thinking, God forgive me. I knew all sorts of scientific and technical theories existed about infinity, but I knew they weren't right. I firmly believed that infinity was beyond the comprehension of the human mind. The most brilliant brains on earth could never explain it, I just knew they couldn't. And that in itself was terribly frightening.

I was told to put these thoughts out of my head and rely on belief and faith. That wasn't good enough. Belief and faith are blind. To me, it was like having a teacher tell you two and two equals five. You may believe that, if you know no better, but you only have their word for it. Where was the proof? I wasn't interested in faith, I wanted knowledge with a capital 'K'. Surely, I thought, there had to be a truth behind all these questions swirling around inside me. And that truth must be universal.

Maybe we were just a chemical accident, as atheists believe – animals who have reached a certain level of intellectual capacity through the trial and error of evolution. I couldn't really accept that. It made everything seem so pointless and futile. You only had to look at the complexity of a flower, the birth of a baby, or study sub-atomic particles and the way they mirror the macrocosm of the universe to see there is definitely a plan and purpose to creation. Of that I was, and am, sure.

In my twenties a girlfriend and her mother took me to a spiritualist meeting while I was on leave from the Army. To be frank, I didn't particularly want to go. It was as much an interest in the girl as curiosity about mediums that got me there. At that time it didn't particularly mean anything to me.

This man, who I had never seen before, stood up and passed various messages to people. Suddenly, he said, 'I have something for a young man at the back,' and he pointed to me.

'I can see a tall man in a white coat standing by you. He has something around his neck.'

I took this to be my grandfather, in his doctors' garb and with a stethoscope.

'He is saying that you're at the bottom rung of a ladder,'

he continued, 'and if you hang on to it you'll get to the top. And there are two maiden aunts looking after you.' He paused and added, 'Three problems will affect your life. Two will be solved for you, the other you must solve yourself.'

The medium went on to say some other things, all of which eventually made sense and turned out to be quite meaningful to me. I was impressed by this, but didn't follow it up. Life dragged me away and I put it to the back of my mind.

Later, when I was living with my first family in our lovely old Queen Anne house in Islington, I had a number of table-rapping sessions. We would write out the alphabet, and the words 'yes' and 'no', on scraps of paper and lay them in a circle on a tabletop. Then four or five of us put our fingers on a wine glass in the centre and asked if there was anybody there.

We got some very positive results, and we certainly weren't messing about. On one occasion a message came through from the actor Sabu, the 'elephant boy', asking us to make a film of his life! Why he of all people should have contacted us is a mystery. Although the idea of a filmed biography is actually quite an interesting one. He had an extraordinary life, and ended up an alcoholic, I believe.

Another time we settled down at the table and almost instantly got K-I-L-L. This was shocking, but nevertheless we asked who was trying to come through. The reply was, *Kill, kill, kill.* After a certain amount of gibberish this entity started to answer our questions more logically.

'Are you there?' I asked.

Yes.

'Where are you?'

In the attic. There was indeed a flat at the top of the house converted from an attic.

Half an hour or so of questioning this vehement spirit revealed a sordid story. Apparently, he was some kind of ostler who had lived in the attic with his wife. He was unfaithful to her and she murdered him. When he got to this part of the tale the message *kill her, kill her, kill her* was repeated over and over again. Then it became *kill the dog*, presumably a reference to the little Yorkshire terrier we had at the time. From that night, strangely, the animal would never again venture upstairs. And our cleaning lady had always hated it up there and couldn't be induced to enter the flat at any price. It was a frightening experience.

Shortly afterwards, we left the house – the move was planned, it had nothing to do with this – and one of the floors collapsed. But almost as soon as we contacted this spirit, or whatever it was, the atmosphere in Colebrook Row deteriorated and we found the place much less welcoming than it had been. Someone said they'd heard footsteps in this flat. Personally, I had no such experience, but I didn't like the feel of the house from that moment.

Make of it what you will.

After about ten years in *Coronation Street*, and having taken full advantage of the opportunities for misbehaviour offered by the swinging sixties, the feeling of dissatisfaction with my life was really beginning to trouble me. I still had this sense of something missing. I began to look around for ways to fill the void, and did a great deal of reading on subjects like yoga and Buddhism. I felt an affinity with these disciplines, and got a warmth from them I had never received from the Church.

At about this time a friend suggested I attend a meeting being held in Dulwich by a homoeopathic practitioner called Dr Maugham. Having heard intriguing and remarkable things about this man, I gladly went.

The meeting took place in his waiting room, which was packed to capacity; there must have been fifty or sixty people there. Dr Maugham, who was reputedly ninety years old, had a long, grey beard and sparkling, intelligent brown eyes.

There was no formality. He simply came in, sat down and began to talk. He spoke on a wide range of subjects but made no mention of religion. It was absolutely riveting.

Then the room was darkened and he told us all to meditate. 'Visualise a circle of light around us all,' he said, 'this will protect us. Sit straight, balance your breathing, put your consciousness in the centre of your brows.' He told us to imagine it was a lovely day and we were sitting on a log in a forest clearing.

I tried this and felt a wonderful sense of peace.

After about twenty minutes of total silence we all opened our eyes again and he asked if anyone had anything to report. People came out with the most incredible things; of how they had seen things and met people while in the meditative state. Following this he encouraged questions from the floor, questions on any subject whatsoever, and his answers were always interesting and full of wisdom.

He was an adept, open man, a man who had reached an amazing level of awareness and consciousness. He was the kind of master you are very fortunate to meet in this life. And the sort you only find when you are ready and deserving of their guidance.

I went to see him on two or three further occasions, and subsequently consulted him purely homoeopathically. He asked me what the trouble was and I said, 'I feel depleted physically, mentally and spiritually.' He gave me some homoeopathic treatment and I went home.

That night I had a very vivid dream. He was sitting at the desk in his untidy old study and said to me, 'You're very welcome to come and join us, Bill.' It was strange, but very, very clear.

So I went to see him again. As I walked into his surgery he smiled at me and said, 'Did you get my message?'

I was staggered. 'Yes,' I said.

Then he repeated what had been said in the dream: 'You're very welcome to come and join us, Bill.'

Dr Maugham was the leader of the Druid Order.

Now, the Druid Order is widely misunderstood, and it isn't for everybody. I would say the test of any of these weird cults we hear so much about these days is whether they try to get money out of you and make life a misery if you want to leave. The Druids are exactly the opposite. They never ask for any material contribution and you have to fight your way in. I was welcomed from the start, but it soon became apparent that if you do not or cannot undertake the necessary work, attend the meetings and apply yourself, you go.

A common misconception about Druidism is that it's at odds with Christianity. This is not so; it's just as pro Christianity as anything else. People say it's pagan. It isn't. It talks about Christ, and actually gives one a better understanding of what Christ is than any Christian religion I know.

Another myth is that modern Druidism is a Victorian creation. No. The Druid Order is very ancient indeed. It was already old when the Romans conquered this country. There was a revival of interest in Victorian times, it's true, but the thread has been continuous. When the Romans arrived they persecuted the Druids and drove them underground. The Christians were hardly more sympathetic. The order had to exist as a secret society until comparatively recent times.

Druidism is not a religion, it is a philosophy. I'm not going to go into it in great detail because it's an esoteric school, and an esoteric school *par excellence*, but basically it teaches you how to search for the truth. You could study with them and then embrace Judaism, Christianity, Islam, atheism or anything else you can think of, and still apply Druidic principles. Because it teaches how to evolve yourself and how to look for the truth wherever it may be found.

Looking for the truth sounds simple. But how many people are able to rid themselves of bias, prejudice, opinions, belief, faith and all the other trappings picked up as we go through life? How many people can strip themselves clean, approach new ideas with a fresh look and assess them objectively? Studying with the Druids was only a step on the path of my quest for greater knowledge. I studied in many other areas and gradually I came to certain realisations or understandings.

Our chattering minds and turbulent emotions have to be bypassed in order to see reality for what it is. This is where meditation comes in.

The ultimate purpose of meditation is to open up the seven sacred energy centres, called chakras, located in our bodies. These relate directly to the endocrine glands. The object is to release the free flow of the life force, kundalini, which resides at the base of the spine. Raising one's kundalini leads to enlightenment. This can only be done at a high level and under guidance.

Really good healers are mediums for these powers, but they have to be very careful – they can deplete themselves. I know a wonderful healer called Arthur Johnson, and you can feel the warmth of this healing power radiating from his hands.

The medical profession should accept the fact that healing works and can assist people in all sorts of ways. Genuine healers, if they were brought into the medical mainstream, could do really good work.

The earth has chakras, or energy centres just like the human body. Stonehenge is one, as are the pyramids in Egypt and Mexico. These structures were built by men with direct cognition. That is why Stonehenge, for instance, is a perfect instrument for assessing planetary positions. These men had knowledge that was in some ways greater than we have now. Stonehenge is an astrological observatory, but also an energy centre that was used to initiate seekers hoping eventually to become adepts.

When Christianity came along it built its first churches on many of these energy points. And, like chakras, these points are linked by channels, called ley lines, which is why the churches always had to be aligned in a specific way. This was in order to properly channel and exploit the magnetic energy that flowed along the leys. When you walk into old churches they are still alive with this energy. You can feel it. Stone has a living quality to it. Modern churches, built sometimes of concrete and rarely aligned correctly, have a marked absence of this energy.

Some years ago I received a certain amount of coverage in the media because I celebrated the Summer Solstice at Stonehenge. People ask me why I don't still do this. It is because that was only a part of my search for knowledge. I have since gone on and studied in other places in my search for the truth, or quest for the Holy Grail. You have to eventually do things in your own way from your own stand point and understanding. I did a most enjoyable series of lectures with Dr Douglas Baker a fascinating man, who has a philosophy school in Essenden, and I hope to publish a book covering this subject in greater detail.

I would venture to suggest that someone like Prince Charles, whose own voyage of spiritual discovery has also been widely misinterpreted and ridiculed, will know about these things. I'm sure he would speak more freely and publicly on the subject if he thought he would get a fair hearing. And he has to be careful because one day he will be the head of the Church of England. I think he is eminently suitable for this role, and to be king, because apart from being an intelligent man he has an understanding beyond the normal. This will make him an ideal head of both State and Church.

People talk about the lucky accident of birth. There's no such thing. You deserve the position you are born into by earning it. People are not born into royalty for no reason.

At least 50 per cent of the world's population believes in reincarnation. Unfortunately many erroneously believe that reincarnation means you can come back as a beetle or other animal. A human spirit remains a human spirit always.

A lot of people think a belief in reincarnation is a cop-out — no need to bother now because I'll be coming round again, that sort of thing. But it is quite the reverse. You are held totally responsible and will pay the price for, or reap the reward of, all your actions. This is called karma. Our progress and future lives are in our own hands.

For purely selfish reasons it's not in our interests to behave badly. Being harmful to others ensures being reborn into a vicious environment and having harm done to us. If you improve yourself one iota you've improved the whole human race because you're a member of it. Self-improvement is what life is about. On the most profound level people are responsible for themselves and for their actions.

The whole purpose of being on this planet is spiritual growth.

Of course, we are all weak, and I don't always practice everything I preach. The good news, I came to realise, is that we go on. Death isn't the end of everything. There is a purpose.

I am in the Church of England and I wish to stay within the Church of England but the church to survive has to change.

The church has become lost in sectarian and theological argument and is no longer spiritually based. That is why only 2 per cent of the country attend.

The message of Christ was simple, love and forgiveness. What does it matter if another interprets the scriptures differently, wants women priests, let them walk alongside and peacefully co-exist.

The church only needs to look at its own history. The Bible is a compilation of holy works selected by the popes and cardinals up to the fifth century. Some of those that had been rejected were discovered in an old jar at Nag Hammadi in 1945. They included many sayings of Jesus and had been written nearer to the time of his presence than the gospels included in the Bible.

Why, along with other works, had they been rejected? For the same reason that the church today will not accept them. Because they talk about the spiritual realms, that each human being is an incarnated spirit. That we can all contact and work with our own spiritual selves and that the purpose of existence is spiritual growth. We are all spirits in the process of development.

When we contact our spiritual selves we become peace loving. If everyone were to stop and do this the problems in the former Yugoslavia, Northern Ireland, South Africa, and of violent crime generally would be resolved. Peace cannot be imposed from the outside it must come from within.

This of course is a threat to the structure of the church and the power of the priests. It should not be the role of the priests to intervene between us and God but rather that they should step aside and teach us how to evolve and contact our own spiritual selves. But they for the most part do not now understand the true nature of things and would not want to relinquish their power.

The reason people are turning to cults is because they are becoming spiritually aware and the church is not giving them the teaching they require. They will continue to fall away from the established church unless it looks to its own background and changes its teaching. If it does then it will flourish for another two thousand years, if it does not then there will be a new Christian church based on love and forgiveness and that the human soul evolves through progressive incarnations.

There have been many Christian sects in the past that have done this, the Essenes, the Gnostics and the Cathars but they were branded heretics and persecuted as they were a threat to the power of the church of Rome.

The new church would teach the method and process of death, and after, thereby removing fear. That Christ is the most highly evolved spiritual being at the head of a hierarchy that governs our solar system.

These have been secret teachings but we are now ready for them and the church must accept it. The time has come for the new age.

Fourteen

One of the great discoveries I have made while pursuing the quest for enlightenment has been the universal and timeless efficacy of astrology.

I don't mean astrology as most people understand it from newspapers and magazines, which deals exclusively with sun signs and paints on far too broad a canvas to be of any real significance.

True astrology shows that the planets are living entities, and that it isn't only gravitational forces that emanate from them, but magnetic and spiritual forces. When and where you are born makes you a unique product of that moment and that place. Only someone born at exactly the same moment in exactly the same place would have an identical astrological chart to your own.

When I started to study astrology, the hardest part, and the thing that took me the longest, was the drawing up of the charts. This involves plotting the position of the planets in the heavens at the time of the subject's birth using logarithms. For the first time in my life I realised logarithms had a useful purpose! Drawing up a chart, getting all the houses and planets right and working out their aspects, used to take me an evening before I even got to interpreting the chart. It's well said that drawing up the chart is a craft, interpreting it is an art.

I took a twelve-month course with The Faculty of Astro-logical Studies, and at the end of it passed an examination which means I'm capable of putting together and interpreting a chart – doing astro-analysis as it's called. As I went along with these studies, I grew to appreciate the greater depths and insights astrology allows the student, and what a truly won-drous thing it is. And, as with meditation, an understanding of astrological principles teaches you an enormous amount about yourself as well as other people.

When my colleagues on *Coronation Street* heard I was proficient in astrology quite a few of them asked me to cast their charts. I'm pleased to say they were suitably impressed and often referred to them years later.

I remember someone at Granda coming to me and asking if I would do a chart for his Dutch girlfriend. When he got it, he said, 'You're absolutely brilliant. You *must* have met her, it's amazingly accurate.' 'It's not *me* that's brilliant,' I told him, 'it's astrology.' And I was fortunate in that she had aspects in her chart that made her a fairly strong character, which always makes the task a little easier.

Being a good astrologer is dependent upon having the ability to interpret, and after a while your intuition starts to kick in. A really good astrologer can bring his or her own understanding to interpretation, and can add an element beyond what's on the pieces of paper in front of them.

Because you are a product of your time – that imprint is laid upon you the instant you were born – the transits of the planets will give you good and bad phases. There's no doubt about this. Sara is a Scorpio, I'm a Taurean, and Pluto has been in her sign and in opposition to mine for a few years now. And it is giving us both a right working over, I can tell you. It moves away this year, thank goodness. But these sorts of aspects are what's meant when people talk about the divinatory side of astrology. In the sense that if you're having a hard time, or a positive one, you can say, 'Oh yes, that's why.'

You can also look at the nature of the harmony, or other-wise, to be expected between two people. In a marriage or business partnership, for example. You can tell if two people are going to be a good couple. Employing sun signs alone for this is far too simplistic. Someone can have their sun in Capricorn but all the other planets in Aries, so although they are officially Capricornian they will probably behave more like an Aries.

Sceptical or frivolous people might say, 'All right, what sign am I then? Come on, do your bit!' I refuse to play that game. But I can say, 'Well, you seem to have a lot of earth in you', or a lot of fire or one of the other elements. Very few people are truly typical of their sign. Whatever their sun sign may be, and granted the sun is the major influence, there are still nine planets to temper this. The positioning of the moon in their chart, their ascendant and the placement of the other planets, all build up a picture considerably more subtle than the sun sign alone.

Astrology informs you. I often relate it to a game of bridge. Astrology will tell you the hand you've been dealt and the abilities of the other players. But you play the game. A lot of people think astrology will do things for them; actually fashion the future in some way. In reality it's only an indicator. It will no more map out your future than a speedometer will drive your car for you. Astrology points, it does not direct. A bit like a compass. The element of free-will determines how you actually live your life, but knowing what general astrological 'weather' is coming up gives you a basis on how to make decisions about the future.

Sometimes you come across people with seemingly very negative charts. Of course you don't say to them, 'Oh, it looks like you're going to be murdered,' or something. Apart from being thoroughly unethical, that response indicates a basic misunderstanding of the subject. Some of the greatest people, the highest achievers, have overcome what are on the face of it very bad charts. So it's not fatalistic in that sense. It just tells you, 'This is what you are, these are the circumstance you're going through, now it's up to you.' And being forewarned is being forearmed.

But I stress again that interpretation is all. In my own chart, for example, I have a configuration called a grand trine, which on the face of it means that everything will be given to you; all life's goodies on a plate. But it could be you are a very weak, ineffectual person born to a wealthy parent, and quite capable of frittering away your fortune.

I've also got sun-squared Saturn, which is one of the worst things you can have. Saturn is like the stern headmaster, and I always feel he's waiting to tap me on the shoulder and say, 'Now come on, what do you think you're doing here?' Saturn makes you pay for things, in all sorts of ways. Therefore, although I have achieved a great deal in my chosen profession, it's always been at the expense of hard work and often not a little heartache. *Coronation Street* came along, and it's given me many years of good employment and a great deal of satisfaction, but I had to be truly deserving, and must keep giving of my best to maintain it.

Generally speaking, astrology falls into two categories – divinatory and character assessment, although the two cross over to a great extent. It's absolutely spot-on when it comes to character. Say you've got, as I have, this sun-squared Saturn, and later you see that Pluto has worked its way through. In retrospect you can see why the previous three-or four-year period was such a hard time, and why nothing came easily.

There again, it isn't like saying, 'On Thursday you're going to be run over by a bus'. But what you might say is that Mercury, to do with movement, and Mars, to do with quick activity, are badly aspected in your third house so you're probably going to be accident prone. You can see that sort of thing. And if you're aware of it and you make yourself walk about more slowly, you will not be run over by the bus. The divination side is not fixed, permanent or immovably preordained. You can overcome it.

I hope to write a book on astrology – I have in fact made a start on it – and my intention is to make it easier for people to interpret charts. I don't kid myself that this is an easy task, but I'm pretty good at simplifying and explaining things and I'm trying to make it not too technical. The signs – how they're made up – the houses, the planets and what the character of each house and planet and sign is.

One thing that irritates me is that the level of public discussion on astrology – and on most esoteric subjects in fact – is so abysmally low. I took part in a television debate between three astronomers and three astrologers. As usual, the astronomers were disdainful, condescending and highly critical about the subject of astrology.

But we won that debate hands down because not one of the astronomers had bothered to study astrology. They had done what most people do, dismissed it out of hand while being almost totally ignorant of how it works. One of them said, 'I think astrology's rubbish.' It transpired that what he meant was, 'The little bit I know is rubbish.' And he was probably right.

One of the big criticisms astronomers have of astrology is that when the art as we know it was created by the Chaldeans, the position of the constellations was different to the way it is now – over that immense period of time things have moved on and the houses are now in the 'wrong' position. They slam astrology on the erroneous assumption that we don't know that or take it into account. This is what the New Age of Aquarius is about. It is taking over from Pisces the place that was originally held by Aries.

When we came up with arguments that countered their prejudices they were totally floored. Brilliant though they are as astronomers, they could not argue against astrology because they didn't know a thing about it. Indeed one of them admitted as much after the programme.

In fact, astronomy grew out of astrology's need for more

accurate information about the planets. Not so long ago, the two disciplines were referred to in the same breath.

Anybody who studies astrology with an open mind will realise its validity and the practical applications it has in all levels of everyday life. I don't have much time for people who dismiss astrology without studying it. And I know that those who have studied it don't dismiss it.

Of course it's only fair to acknowledge that there are charlatans who attached themselves, leech-like, to all the subjects I have discussed here. This is very pertinent as I write, because the siege of the religious commune headed by David Koresh, a man who called himself Jesus Christ, has just ended so tragically in Waco, Texas.

Some people are now finding that traditional churches are not satisfying their spiritual needs. These people are sincerely searching to fill a spiritual void in their life, as I was. And, as I didn't, they don't know what it is they're looking for. They are easy prey for some of these cults. And the people who run them have a sort of magnetism. They probably have a lot of esoteric knowledge, and when someone acquires this knowledge, at any level, they can break through and become an adept, or they can go the dark way. When Jesus was tempted in the wilderness the devil told him he could have all the material things he wanted. He had that choice and overcame it. We all have that choice too.

You have to be very wary once you step on the path of enlightenment. This is why the exoteric religions, the Church of England and so on, warn against these cults.

But this is no reason not to embark on the journey. We are made up of the spiritual, the mental, the emotional and the physical – as represented by the elements fire, air, earth, ether and water – and we have to harmonise them. And when we do, we become healthier, live longer and stand a far better chance of achieving happiness. Of course, there are pitfalls. And along the way one must cast off a lot of spiritual and emotional baggage picked up over the years.

But there's a wonderful old saying: 'Shatter your ideals on the rock of truth.'

Many of the things I have said here will strike the casual reader as strange. Those already on the path to enlightenment will be aware of the truth in what I say. Others will scoff.

I would only remind you of another ancient adage: 'He who seeks will find.' And if you don't seek you won't find.

Fifteen

I was born into a solid middle-class home. The son of a doctor, I attended a boarding school and generally enjoyed the advantages of a comfortable upbringing. Although we were never a particularly political family, it would be accurate to say we were natural Tories.

Ilkeston, my birthplace, was a mining town. There were thriving pits all around and one of the boys I played with as a child was the son of a miner. My father was often called to attend accidents in the mine. And although, perhaps surprisingly, we knew of quite a lot of Tory-voting miners, our political leanings could be said to go against the norm for the area. In fact, at one general election my parents voted Labour. So there was no question of our being party members or diehard activists.

My mother had no interest in politics at all. My father was hardly more interested. Which seems an odd thing to say, considering he was a Conservative member of the local council at one point. He did this purely because he was approached – they hadn't got anybody else – and it was a totally safe seat. The story goes that he said, 'Well all right, just so long as I don't have to go out electioneering.' He was elected, did his bit for one session, didn't particularly like it and withdrew.

Speaking for myself, I was always more interested in deeper

issues. To some people, for whom politics is everything, that may appear almost offensive. But to me politics deal more with the physical aspects of life and I was always more concerned with the metaphysical. I voted Conservative as a reactionary. No thought was given to it. I just did it because that's the way it was.

But as I got deeper into thinking and reading about the esoteric side of life I found myself looking at the material world and assessing what had been automatic responses. I began applying the philosophy I mentioned earlier; I examined my opinions and beliefs and endeavoured to view the political spectrum in an objective way.

I started with Communism. Almost any sincerely held ideal is good in its concept, and I could see that for countries bled dry by an elite wealthy class or fascist dictators, Communism was right and revolution probably the only way. But it seemed to me to have destruction in-built because it was atheistic. Second, human nature has not got to the point where a single, totalitarian party, should be allowed to govern. As we've now seen, after the collapse of Communism, the corruption, the secret police, the torture, the lack of individual freedom and so on, were all endemic under that system. On top of that, it stultified individual enterprise. So although Communism, maybe right and proper in some places, I didn't see it as something good in the long run.

Socialism was only really a step out of Communism towards democracy, as far as I was concerned, or the acceptable face of Communism and was painted with the same brush. It also believed in central government doing everything for you, in controlling from the centre and telling you what to do. This is fine for the old, the infirm and people who aren't able to look after themselves. But what I was looking for, in my new philosophy which says you are responsible for your actions, was a society where I had freedom to express myself. A society, moreover, that was law-abiding, financially sound and had compassion towards the less fortunate.

The only party that fitted the bill was the Conservatives.

I'm talking about basic philosophies here. What people tend to do in following party lines is take up an ideology and defend it to the death. This is not right. Politicians – men and women – are not infallible. No political party is perfect. It needs to adjust, grow, and rectify the inevitable mistakes it will make. I believe the Conservatives have this capability and so I came back to them quite happily. I vote for the Conservative party with a clear conscience.

I thought Margaret Thatcher was a sincere, honest, strong and courageous leader. I know a lot of people think otherwise, but that was my view. She was well-meaning and trying to take the country forward to where it would be, law-abiding and prosperous. And she was shedding the shackles of Socialism where it held things down. So, come the 1983 election, I decided to 'come out'.

For an actor, standing up and expressing a political opinion can be a dangerous thing to do, because you are bound to automatically alienate 50 per cent of the population. Certainly those who are politically concerned, and opposed to your views, will go off you. And if you're a character in a television drama serial, and your politics are known, you are bound to upset some people. For this reason, a lot of actors refuse to commit themselves.

But two things concerned me. One was that Ken Barlow was regarded as a staunch Socialist in the early days of *Coronation Street*, so it was automatically assumed that I was too. People do tend to link actors and characters together in that way. It didn't concern me too much, but I didn't particularly like it. The other thing was that it looked as though the 1983 election wasn't going to be as clear-cut in its outcome as the previous one. I felt it was right that Margaret Thatcher and the Conservatives should have a further term and decided to contribute.

We had just come to live in Wilmslow, which is a sort of Tunbridge Wells of the North, and the election was some way off. I was invited to a craft exhibition at Wilmslow library – I get invited to things like that a lot – and Neil Hamilton, the local MP, and his wife Christine were there. He was wearing a red bowtie. I said to Sara, 'Surely he isn't . . .' not in Wilmslow. He was very pleasant. We were just polite to each other, nothing more than that. We had photographs taken, looked around the exhibition, and as we were leaving I said to Neil Hamilton, 'If I can be of any help with the election, would you let me know?' I've never seen two faces change so much; their eyes practically popped out of their sockets. He said, 'But I thought you were –' 'No,' I said, 'I'm not.' From then on we became, and remain, close friends. At the time of writing Neil is a minister with the Department of Trade & Industry and I am sure is destined for high office.

After that my phone never stopped. Not only was Neil's agent ringing me to do walkabouts, but also other local MPs – Tom Arnold, Alistair Burt, Ken Hargreaves and Sir Fergus Montgomery – heard I was sympathetic and the next two weeks were taken up solidly making appearances with them too.

I'd come out. And I was a little apprehensive. Quite rightly so in some circumstances. Walking round Bury Market with a Conservative rosette on was very different to opening a shop where all the people *want* to see you turn up. You live under the impression that everybody loves you. But try walking around Bury Market as a representative of the Conservative party and you suddenly find there are a lot of people who *don't* love you. People shouted things like, 'I'm not going to watch your show any more!' and, 'I never thought you were like this!' Two or three chaps were very aggressive. But on balance, I think I had more people coming up and being affable.

Margaret Thatcher did a rally at Chester and a small group of local supporters, just four or five of us, were invited to meet her beforehand. We had a chat with her and she was quite delightful. She listened to what we had to say and displayed a lovely sense of humour. She spoke about her strident, hard image, and actually asked Sara and I what she could do about it. I said, 'Well, I just wish everyone could meet you.' Because she isn't like her image – indeed she's quite vulnerable in a way, and attractive.

After that I was asked to do after dinner talks to various Conservative associations all over the place, and met a lot of other members of parliament.

Then we got our first invitation to Downing Street, which was really interesting. Mrs Thatcher welcomed us herself and showed us around. She took us into the cabinet room. The Falklands war had recently been fought and she quite openly talked of the debates they had had about it. That was really fascinating. She spoke about how worried she had been, how frightened of the commitment, but how underneath she just knew it had to be done. It was wonderful to walk around Downing Street, to see all the paintings of past prime ministers and hear some of the history of the place.

When we first arrived and Mrs Thatcher approached us, I felt I wanted to say something to her that was sincere but without sounding fawning or flattering. I just wanted to compliment her, because people in her position are battling all day long and I'm sure compliments are thin on the ground. So I said, 'You know, Prime Minister, you seem to have an understanding of people's needs that goes beyond the normal, almost into a spiritual realm. I think it's this that gives you your unerring judgement.' She looked at me with her head tilted on one side for a moment, obviously considering what I'd said, then replied, 'Yes, you're absolutely right.' There was a slight smile on her lips.

What I said was meant. I do feel that, whether it was woman's intuition or whatever, she had a direct line with something. More often than not when things went wrong it was because she wavered to other people's points of view. Whether you agreed with her or not, her own instincts were right.

We were invited to Downing Street a second time the following year, and had another very pleasant and fascinating evening there.

Then Margaret Thatcher came to visit *Coronation Street*. The management knew of my political leanings so I was the one delegated to take her along the Street set. I walked her down to the Rovers' Return, where all the cast were gathered. The visit was supposed to be brief, but she stayed for over thirty minutes, chatting away to everybody. Even those who weren't of her political persuasion said later how delightful she was.

Her dismissal came as a shock. I must say I was deeply upset and felt there had been acts of treachery involved. I think the way she handled her last prime minister's question time, when already it was known that she had been forced to resign, was magnificent.

However, her protégé and chosen successor whom she had elevated so rapidly, John Major, came along and won the next election. I am not being disloyal when I say the victory came as a surprise. There's no doubt the election was won because he came across as a man of the people; his common sense and basic decency shone through.

As part of their campaign the Conservatives held a series of rallies around the country, employing a kind of collapsible theatre set. They were very nervous about these events because they were expensive to mount. The first one was held in Manchester, in a big hangar at the airport, on 19th March, 1992, and I was asked to open it and introduce the Prime Minister. I was petrified about this, but agreed.

So my first meeting with John Major took place just before this rally started. And I found him the most wonderfully charming and sensitive man. We had a long chat with him and he said to Sara about my introduction of him 'Isn't he a clever boy'. Later, Sir Fergus Montgomery, who with his wife Lady Joyce have also become good friends of ours, threw a party at Westminster to which he invited a few celebrities, myself and Sara included. John Major came. He was just going to pop in briefly, but in the event stayed from about 8.30 right through until midnight. We chatted and I found him absolutely straight and very charming. He gave everyone his full attention. I really liked the man. Not only that, I had confidence in him, and respected him.

After the election, and completely out of the blue, we received an invitation to lunch at Chequers on 31st May, 1992.

We decided to go down the night before, and stayed at the Bell House hotel near Beaconsfield, which is very near where I played in *Ivanhoe*. The following day we had to be at Chequers by midday.

At the main gate we were told to go round to a side entrance. We went down a little lane to a small gate, and apart from some armed policemen with flak-jackets and hand-mirrors for looking under the car, we were unaware of any particularly heavy security. Although I'm sure this was intentionally deceptive. Once we got through that, we drove down the gravel driveway into a little walled courtyard with brick walls around it.

As we walked in John Major came rushing up, saying, 'Bill! How are you? I'm so glad to hear you're better.' This in reference to an ulcer I'd had shortly before. He had sent a handwritten note to me in hospital and said he was going to visit me. In the end this wasn't possible but Kenneth Baker – the Home Secretary – came instead. 'And, Sara, how are you?' he said, giving her a big kiss. Then we were led into the main room. Cilla Black, Rocco Forte, Norman Tebbit and one or two others were there. It was not a large lunch party.

A nice surprise was that Mr Major's lovely wife, Norma, turned out to be a great *Coronation Street* fan, and was full of questions about the show.

Chequers is exactly as you imagine it will be, and not unlike one of those country mansions Agatha Christie was so fond of setting her murder mysteries in. We were there until four o'clock. Before we left, John Major mentioned that he had another meeting at four-thirty, and the next day he was off to Europe for a conference. And yet he displayed no sign of tiredness or distraction. My tremendous admiration and respect for him was heightened by that very memorable day at Chequers. I asked him how he managed to cope with everything. He said he had the ability to give total concentration to whatever he was doing. This was apparent as he was talking to us.

I do understand a lot of people don't like the fact that I vote Conservative and am vocal in my support of the party. I respect opposing points of view and am always ready to listen and discuss them with people. I have yet to hear an argument, however, that would make me change my mind. But that doesn't mean I think everything the Conservative party does is right. I can be as critical as anyone when it goes wrong and when it makes the wrong decisions. One isn't blinded by slavish dogma.

What I do dislike are people who come up and shout slogans at you: 'You've climbed to where you are on the back of the workers,' somebody once accused me. I've not climbed on anybody's back. I inherited nothing from my father and became an actor in my own right, and went through a lot of problems, insecurities and difficulties on the way.

One of the great things about democracy, and this country in particular, is our capacity to agree to disagree. In other countries opposition to the status quo can land you in prison or in front of a firing-squad, and revolutions are held in place of elections. We are, I think, fairly civilised in our behaviour. We should value and respect the democracy we have and the freedom of speech it allows us.

Sixteen

The 16th November, 1984, was the worst day of my life.

In July of that year Sara and I had moved into our present home here in Wilmslow. Verity was three, and our new baby, Edwina, just eighteen months.

The week before the 16th Edwina developed a cold and a slight cough. We're always very cautious when it comes to the children so we got the doctor in right away. He prescribed antibiotics. On the 15th, which was a Thursday, I came home from the studio and found Edwina was getting quite hoarse and the cough was no better. The doctor was called again and came along the following morning to take another look at her.

On the Friday night she seemed much improved. Her temperature was down, she was quite calm and peaceful, and it looked as though she was on the mend. Sara and I went out for a Chinese meal that evening, leaving our in-laws to babysit, and got back from the restaurant at around 10.30 p.m. Sara went straight up to see Edwina and she was fine. We pottered around downstairs until 11.20, at which point Sara popped up to the nursery to check again.

A moment later there was a terrible scream.

I dashed upstairs. Sara was desperately trying to rouse Edwina, who seemed lifeless. 'Quick!' I said, 'Call for an ambulance!' I gave Edwina the kiss of life, I smacked her on her back; I tried everything I could think of to revive her. I held her upside down, but there was no sign of life.

It seemed an eternity before the ambulance came. In point of fact it arrived quite quickly, but our anguish and helplessness made the wait appear endless. The paramedics took over and applied all their life-saving skills. Then Sara carried Edwina to the ambulance, I jumped into the car, and we raced to the hospital.

The medical staff did all they could. But it was hopeless. Edwina was dead.

There are no words to describe the utterly devastating sense of loss and shock. No way to convey to anyone who has not experienced the tragedy of the death of a child the all-pervading, overwhelming grief that engulfed us. It was every parent's nightmare, and it was happening to us.

One minute our darling daughter was a perfectly normal, healthy child, running and playing around the house. The next, she was gone. We simply did not believe what was happening, we couldn't take it in.

The worst thing is the feeling of guilt.

It didn't matter that we had done everything that could be expected of caring parents. The fact is you are responsible for your children and they look to you for protection, guidance and succour. We could not shake off the thought that we had let Edwina down in some way.

It was not a cot death. The postmortem showed that one of the tubes to Edwina's lungs, which are so tiny in a baby, had become blocked with catarrh, cutting off the supply of air. The doctor told us that when this happens, short of operating instantly, very little can be done. He said he had even seen a baby die in its mother's arms as a result of this condition.

We went into that weekend in a state of total numbness. The depth of shock we were in was extraordinary. There was this incredible churned-up feeling mixed with indescribable hurt. We talked a little, and just sat together all through the night and the following day. We couldn't eat.

The only thing we could get down were occasional cups of hot chocolate.

It was fortunate that I was just starting two weeks out of *Coronation Street*. We stayed in this limbo for days. Not living, but simply existing, dragging out the hours in blackest despair. I didn't want to go out or see anybody. I couldn't speak on the phone without choking with tears. The grief was a pain, an actual, physical pain inside me. On the third day I remember saying to Sara, 'I can't go on any more. I really can't take this grief.'

We were lucky in that we could talk. And we have a belief, an understanding, that this life is not the end. I know that. Edwina had been taken for a reason, and we knew we would be seeing her again somewhere, some way.

We got to the morning of the funeral and I thought, I'm not going to be able to cope with this. But as I lay there, steeling myself for the awful ordeal the day held, something extraordinary happened. I looked up and saw Edwina, surrounded by a glorious glowing light, like a halo. There was a smile on her little face and she was saying, 'I'm okay.' I *know* I saw this. And although the terrible weight of grief did not go, it did immediately lessen, and I felt a tremendous relaxation and welling-up of strength within me. Sara said exactly the same thing. She, too, felt an easing of this intense, unbearable grief. We seemed to have shared some kind of joint experience which gave us the fortitude to go on. I carried the coffin myself. The service was quiet and dignified and we supported each other through it.

Sara and I continued to talk and share our feelings in the days that followed. And, of course, we talked to Verity and explained the situation as best we could. We came to understand that the positive side was being grateful for the eighteen months we had with Edwina. I think the fact that Sara and I were able to open ourselves to each other so much showed how good a relationship we have. I have tremendous sympathy for anyone who has to go through what we endured, but more so for someone who has no partner to lean on. I was so pleased we *could* talk. People take grief in different ways, and some cannot bring themselves to express their feelings. The danger of not talking is that emotions can become suppressed and bottled-up, which is dangerous.

Gradually, I got to the point where I could face going out again. I still felt terrible, and it was strange driving round in the car and seeing people getting on with their daily lives. The world seemed different to me, and not quite real.

It was quite a while before I could talk about Edwina, or talk to anybody without crying. We did a fair amount of crying and our grief was extreme. But we now have Edwina, as it were, in a separate little capsule of golden memory. And, as I said, we thank God for the time she was with us.

If my relationship with Sara was tested in any way, it passed that test very well. As did my beliefs. Or, rather, my understanding. The knowledge that life goes on and can never be extinguished was a tremendous help to us both. But my heart goes out, and will always go out, to anyone who loses a child. It is a totally devastating experience, and unless you go through it you have no idea.

My colleagues were wonderful, so sympathetic and solicitous; nothing was too much trouble for them in our hour of need. Even the Press behaved well. One reporter came to the door and told us a number of his colleagues were at the gate. What did we want to do? I said, 'Would you please leave us alone,' and they did. That is probably the first and last good word I'll have to say about the Press. But they did behave very honorably.

The letters that poured in from the public were extraordinary. The great wave of love and affection people directed at us definitely strengthened us. It made us realise there are a lot of very good, loving people about. That was truly wonderful. From the letters we got we realised some people have had incredible sufferings; at times like this they write and tell you about such things. I'm a great believer in collective thoughts having an effect, just like the power of prayer, and the sympathy, love and consideration that came our way certainly helped sustain us.

We got letters from people who had suffered similar losses. There were letters from mothers who had lost daughters and sons. Many expressed the most terrible despair. I tried to write back to as many of them as I could. I wrote a lot of letters to a lot of people, and in a way I hope that was a good thing that came out of Edwina's death, because they knew I was speaking from the heart. We had shared something. I would be really happy to think I may have provided some small glimmer of hope to them.

A few weeks prior to Edwina's death, and completely unknown to me of course, Sara was negotiating for me to appear as the subject of *This is Your Life*.

Apparently it's usually the spouse the producers approach, and this can cause problems. I heard a wonderful story, which I like to think isn't apocryphal, about Ronnie Barker. It seems the *This is Your Life* office was conspiring with his wife to get him on the programme and she wrote their telephone number inside a pair of knickers. I don't know what possessed her to do this, but in any event Ronnie found this particular item of underwear, rang the number and blew the whole thing.

There was no danger of this kind of mishap occurring with me because Sara handles the business side of my professional life and she's always making phone calls I know nothing about. In fact, she had been dealing with the producers for several weeks, and actually had a meeting with them the morning of Edwina's death. Then, of course, they dropped the whole thing, and she assumed that was the end of it.

But no, they later came back to her, and when they found she had never mentioned it to me the show was re-scheduled for the 24th September, 1984.

Every so often *This is Your Life* featured someone from *Coronation Street*. I'd been on as a guest at other people's about eight times myself. And I had a feeling that, being the longest-running cast member, it was possible they would eventually get around to me. It wasn't something I actively thought about, or longed for, but it was in the back of my mind. However, having appeared on other people's, I knew what the drill was.

The pattern was always the same. After technical run-through on a Wednesday we would all be herded on to a train and taken to the Thames studio in London. Once there, we would sit having a drink in the hospitality room, located in the bowels of the earth, while the victim was picked up. Then we all trooped on. We would stay overnight in an hotel and get back to Manchester the following day. It was all a bit of a chore, to be honest, because it had to be squeezed into a working week.

So I knew that if the Street's producer, Bill Podmore, came to me and said, 'You're wanted in London on Wednesday evening,' it would have given the game away. But that didn't happen. There was a telethon going on, and Thames said they wanted a group of us from the Street to go on, say a few words and wish this charity event success. I was to be the cast spokesman. This was going to be recorded at about five o'clock in the afternoon on Wednesday, 24th September, at Granada. 'It doesn't matter what you wear,' Bill Podmore said, 'just come in casual clothes.'

Rehearsals finished at about three-thirty that day. It wasn't worth going home, so I shambled around the studio, apparently causing absolute panic. Because, as I was to learn later, for the first time the show was going to be done in a studio at Granada. As I wandered around killing time they were dressing the set, which included a massive picture of me.

There was somebody watching me the whole time, although, of course, I didn't know that. I went to the café and had a cup of tea. Then after that, for want of anything better to do, I walked out to the car-park – that must have had some hearts racing! – and got into my car. I reclined the seat and settled back to listen to Radio 4.

Five o'clock eventually came round and when I went back inside I was surprised to find everyone quite smartly dressed. And there I was in a pullover and slacks. 'Why's everybody dressed up?' I asked. 'Oh, don't worry about that,' somebody said. We went to the back of one of the buildings, where this brief message was supposed to be recorded, and just as I started to say my bit somebody giggled. I looked up and there was Eamon Andrews, wearing an Arab headdress and leading a camel! He came up to me, produced the famous red book and announced, 'William Roache, this is your life.'

This is called the pick-up. Once it was over you get a break in order to ready yourself for the show proper. Sara had brought a change of clothes in for me and I put them on in my dressing room. An hour later I was on stage greeting a stream of relatives and friends they had specially brought in.

That morning I had dropped off Verity at school, as I always did. What I didn't know was that ten minutes later Sara had arrived and picked her up again. Verity was taken to a studio where they filmed her little bit. She was sitting in front of a typewriter wearing a green shade, because I was editing a newspaper in the Street at the time. And of course she later came on stage. Sara was pregnant with William at the time, so we always tell him he had appeared on my *This is Your Life* as well.

My mother, sister and nephew and niece came on, and Sara's mother and father, of course. There were twenty members of the cast of *Coronation Street* there. Then they brought on Gertie Senior, my old Matron from Rydal School, who was ninety in March this year and is still going strong. And I was delighted to see Selwyn Hughes, the friend I had made in the Army, who was the obligatory guest from Australia.

They were then joined by Sandy Lyle, Cyril Smith, Mike Yarwood, Jeffrey Archer, Derek Jameson and

Suzi Quatro. And Brian Blessed told some funny stories about our days in rep together.

We had a jolly nice little get together afterwards and I thoroughly enjoyed it.

You get a red book, but not the one Eamon confronts you with at the pick-up. What happens is that you're sent a copy a few weeks later. It's essentially a photograph album, with your name, the date and Eamon Andrews's signature on the title page. A great souvenir of a marvellous evening.

I've heard strange stories about how much certain people treasure their copy of the red book. Hilda Baker, apparently, had it on its own table in a special holder, with a spotlight shining on it. The first thing visitors saw when they went to her house was this little shrine!

This is Your Life is one of the all-time great television ideas, there's no doubt about that. And in some ways its appeal is similar to that of *Coronation Street*. It's a pleasant programme, a celebration of a person's life. So of course nice people will be coming on and saying nice things. And why not? In this day and age I think that's a good thing. There are those who let it be known they will not appear, but if someone wants to throw a party inviting all my friends and relations, I'm only too happy to come along. There is a sort of package of shows you are invited to as a celebrity and I have enjoyed being on *Through the Keyhole*, *Terry Wogan*, *In the Psychiatrist's Chair* and many others, but the most frightening, and most rewarding, is the *Pro-Celebrity Golf*.

Seventeen

For over thirty years I have been seen by millions of people twice a week, latterly three times a week, and one of the prices of this sort of exposure is publicity. For good or ill, it goes with the job.

Critics are paid to express their opinion. Sometimes that opinion can be hurtful, but you take it. If you are as much in the public eye as the cast of *Coronation Street* you accept that there will be people who like you and people who don't. But you never really become hardened to especially harsh reviews, particularly if they contain an element of inaccuracy, or a personal attack. Often in the green room at Granada people have been in tears, deeply upset at some of the awful lies written about them. But we are all professionals and the philosophy is to let these things go by.

Up to seven or eight years ago the Press, although capable of distortions and inaccuracies, had a sort of rough code of conduct. There was usually some truth in what they said, and generally their behaviour was tolerable.

Then the circulation war heated up and the tabloids concentrated even more on the soaps in order to boost their readership. In the case of *Coronation Street* this feeding frenzy reached its height during the Ken/Deirdre/Mike storyline. We were constantly being requested for interviews during that period, several of which our press office granted, given that some publicity is good. But sometimes, having turned down an interview, you would find the paper concerned running what purported to be one anyway. On closer examination it turned out to be cobbled together from bits and pieces that had appeared elsewhere. And usually the facts were all wrong. If we asked them about this they'd say, 'Well, if you'd done the interview in the first place we could have got it right. Why not give us one now?' Another ploy was to run some piece of nonsense and credit it to 'an insider', which is the tabloids' code for 'We made it up'.

The Press seemed more and more concerned with sensation and less and less with the truth.

In 1986 a journalist interviewed me about my life and family, and the material was subsequently published as a series in the *Star*. I had no complaint about that; it was a good series and accurately reproduced what I said. I did some more interviews the following year and the journalist concerned eventually sold them to the *Sun*. This was quite a different kettle of fish. The article had been changed and distorted, and it contained a nasty story about Jean Alexander which was completely fabricated.

I wrote to the *Sun* complaining about this and asking for an apology. They said we could write a correction ourselves. We did, but they didn't run it. They just made constant excuses, obviously with the intention of wearing us down to the point where we gave up. In the event, that's what happened. This is another tabloid trick. And in this case they knew the articles contained nothing really specific enough to go to the law about. That experience left me very wary.

When the Ken/Deirdre bust-up came along there was a scene in which I said to her, 'You think I'm boring, don't you?' Of course, 'Boring Barlow' became an alliteration and started to appear in headlines everywhere. Boring was the adjective they applied to Ken virtually every time he was mentioned. As a label, it stuck, and I didn't like this very much. Because you could take 90 per cent of the characters in the Street in isolation and call them boring. You can call *anybody* boring. In fact I remember a readers' poll in one of the newspapers in which Terry Wogan topped the lists of both most exciting and most boring person on television. He won both categories!

I got talked about as being boring so much that maybe a new definition of the word is that everybody talks about you all the time. Anyway, it became a piece of silliness I felt sure would blow over, given time.

Enter journalist Ken Irwin. Now, when the very first episode of *Coronation Street* went out, he reviewed the show and said it would never last. He poured scorn on it. As the years passed, and the Street maintained its great popularity, Irwin tried to make a joke about this hasty and inaccurate judgement. Indeed, as he climbed the ladder of tabloid journalism, he billed himself as 'The friend of the Street'. This came as quite a surprise to me as I had never particularly trusted the man. And certainly he had no more of an inside track on the programme than a lot of others.

In November, 1990, *The Sun* announced that it was going to publish a series of features by Irwin 'celebrating' *Coronation Street*. The first of these was about Julie Goodyear, and it proved quite nasty. It was full of unpleasant, unsubstantiated gossip, and raked over the ashes of certain things she had suffered in the past. At the end of this piece it said the next day's article was going to be about me, although I had not given Irwin an interview.

I don't normally take *The Sun*, but I bought a copy the following morning because I was in it. I read the article and was absolutely devastated. A lot of it was what the newspaper industry calls a scissors and paste job – a ragbag of odds and sods from the files – and the rest was pure poison.

In his piece about Julie Goodyear, and a later article on Johnny Briggs, Irwin referred to them as Julie and Johnny. With me, it was 'Roache'. The whole tone was totally demeaning. But some of the things he said went way beyond acceptable opinion, indeed they were presented as fact, albeit without sources quoted. He said I was hated by the cast. He said I'd been up for the sack more times than anybody in the Street. He said I was a joke with the writers and couldn't do my job properly. He even said that in the Ken/Deirdre/Mike storyline I had to be carried by Ann and Johnny.

He went on to say I was as boring and smug in real life as the character I play in the Street. He dusted off all the allegations that had previously been made about my activities in the sixties. This in particular was extremely embarrassing and unpleasant, not only for me, but also my family and friends.

None of this was presented as his personal point of view; he claimed to be relaying information from various unnamed 'insiders'. He implied that everything in the article came from conversations he had with producers, writers and members of the cast. This wasn't a 'celebration' of my contribution to *Coronation Street* – it was an attempt at character assassination.

That article knocked me for six. When I got into work that day I made straight for my dressing room. I felt so humiliated and tainted I couldn't face anyone. I was worried sick everybody would think I was no good at my job. *The Sun* has the biggest readership of any daily newspaper in the country – a sad reflection on the tastes of a sizeable proportion of our fellow citizens – and I was only too aware that millions of people were reading these horrible things about me.

Of course the public tends to believe what they read in the Press. Even if it's later refuted, there's this business of 'No smoke without fire.' And when a correction or apology is published statistics show that for every hundred people who read the original article only 12 per cent read the rectification.

I was very, very upset. What had been written affected me, my family, my friends and my professional standing.

It wasn't right or just and I determined to do something about it.

I went to see Granada's company secretary, Alistair Mutch, who agreed with me that it was a scurrilous and potentially damaging piece of journalism. Alistair suggested Granada's lawyers, Goodman & Co, should look it over. Subsequently a member of their staff rang me and we discussed the situation at some length.

'Yes,' he said, 'it is very defamatory, and yes, you could take it to court and would probably win. But we don't recommend that you do.'

I said, 'I assume you always say it isn't worth going ahead with libel?'

'That's right. The trouble is that not only do you suffer the indignities of a court case, you also run the risk of even more people reading it. Then, as it's in front of a jury, you are never a 100 per cent sure you're going to win.

Granada has a policy of never backing anyone in a libel case. I think that policy is correct, but it meant I would be going it alone if I went ahead and sued.

'So what you're saying,' I put to this man from Goodman's, 'is that the papers can libel anyone they like and be almost certain of getting away with it?'

He went on to tell me that nine out of ten such cases fall away for lack of funds, or fear on the plaintiff's part about what they are going to have to go through.

This hit a chord in me. I was not going to give in for either of those reasons. I felt a gross injustice had been done, and was permanently being done, because the system and the newspapers put so many obstacles in the way of the offended party.

I understood why Goodman's advised against suing. But the underlying thought in me was that it had to be done. I knew it would be a high-profile case, and being a very shy and private person that was not a prospect to cherish. The thought of exposure to this sort of thing was very daunting.

However, this article was untrue – it was basically the untruth that got me – and I hated the fact that these papers laughingly got away with it all the time and that they were getting worse and worse.

So it was with resolve, but quite a bit of trepidation, that I approached the country's leading libel lawyer, Peter Carter-Ruck. He was sent a copy of the article and rang me to say, 'This is outrageous, and typical of the muck-raking of a section of the Press. You have as strong a case as I've seen. I give you an 80 per cent chance of winning, which is the highest I give to any libel.'

He agreed to take the case. If I had any tendency to waver, this made up my mind for me. When one of the profession's top experts in libel tells you your case has a high possibility of succeeding you respect that opinion.

The wheels were set in motion.

I went along to see Mr Carter-Ruck in his offices at Holborn. He told me that we needed to arrange witnesses to appear on my behalf, and to obtain statements from my colleagues refuting the allegations in the article. It was a productive and encouraging meeting.

My intention was to catch the train back to Manchester afterwards and I decided to walk to Euston. When I arrived the train was in, but the gates were closed, so I joined the end of the queue. I was standing there reading a newspaper when someone came up behind me and said, 'Hello.' I turned round.

It was Ken Irwin.

I was flabbergasted. Not only at the absolutely incredible coincidence of running into the very man I had just been talking about suing, but at his brass neck for coming up and talking to me. It was a long queue. Had he been twenty or so places ahead of me or behind me it would have been slightly less of a coincidence. But this beggared belief.

Peter Carter-Ruck had warned me not to discuss the case

with anyone, but under the circumstances I couldn't resist saying *something*.

'I'm absolutely horrified by that article you wrote,' I said.

'What article?'

'You know full well what article. I think it's the worst thing that's ever been written about me and I'm taking action.'

'Not against me, I hope.' Then he added something like, 'Well, you know the sort of thing the papers want.'

'My solicitors will be dealing with that,' I informed him and turned my back.

Even then he tried to make small talk. He pointed to something in his newspapers and tried to get me to comment on it. I ignored him, and shortly after that the queue moved on to the train and he disappeared into the crowd.

It was quite extraordinary.

Lindsay Moffett was the solicitor Peter Carter-Ruck deputised to work with me, and she was easy to work with and delightful. We got some witnesses from the cast, including Amanda Barrie, Johnny Briggs, Bill Waddington, Michael Levell and Betty Driver, and the statements began to come in. If nothing else came out of the case, I got some wonderfully glowing testimonials from my colleagues and I was very, very grateful to them.

One thing I don't like is disturbing other people, and having members of the cast come down to London was going to be very disruptive to the schedules. But Granada's management were completely understanding and really went out of their way to accommodate us.

Preparation for the case progressed and I began to understand why legal proceedings can take so long. There was an enormous amount of work to do. And the bills were mounting all the time.

A letter was sent to Kelvin McKenzie, editor of *The Sun*, offering him the opportunity to apologise for the libel and pay our costs. No reply was forthcoming so we went ahead with the serving of writs.

We finally got a date for the case to go into the High Court – 29th October, 1991 – almost exactly a year after the article was published. The judge was to be Chief Justice Waterhouse, the venue Court 13. Our barrister was Mr Charles Gray QC, assisted by a junior called Tom Shields. We had a highly experienced team.

The case was against News Group Newspapers Ltd, publishers of *The Sun*, Kelvin McKenzie and Ken Irwin.

Oddly enough, *The Sun*'s lawyers in the case were Farrar and Co, who are also the Queen's lawyers. It struck me as ironic that they should act for a newspaper which regularly runs stories knocking royalty.

The Sun paid £25,000 into court in September. This was the point where, for the first time, I understood what a payment into court meant. If I chose to take that money the case would be cancelled, the defence would make an apology and my costs to date paid by the newspaper. That would be an end to the matter.

It seemed to me that in terms of punishing the paper, which was one of my major motivations, the sum was laughable. What was £25,000 to a paper that regularly paid people £50,000 for 'kiss-and-tell' stories? They stood to make far more than that from the increased circulation the case's publicity would inevitably bring. Peter Carter-Ruck also thought the figure totally inadequate.

He then explained that if we were awarded damages above £25,000 all was well and good. But if the damages were the same as or below £25,000, I would be liable to pay both side's costs from the time the payment was made into court.

This sent a chill through me. But I was beginning to see that libel is a bit like poker. Money represented the seriousness of the libel. I really didn't mind about the amount in damages I got and would have been happy with something like five to ten thousand pounds. But I wanted the paper to have to pay as much as possible in order to make them think about their behaviour.

Peter said that had they paid into court something like £75,000 or £100,000 he would have been bound to advise me to accept it because that was into the risk area. So, following my feelings, and Peter Carter-Ruck's advice, I decided to refuse the £25,000.

On we went. First, we had to go through a process called discoveries, where both sides show all the evidence they are going to produce. A tremendous amount of work goes on even at this early stage, and already the legal costs were piling up. It all gets very frightening. I don't like going to law, I really don't, and never had before. If asked, I would offer the advice that you should never go to law unless you absolutely have to, but if you have to, get the best representation and go through with it. There's no point in half-hearted bluffs.

In October *The Sun* increased to £50,000 the amount paid into court. By now we were all geared-up and ready to go, and in any event Peter Carter-Ruck still considered the sum inadequate.

We had a meeting in Charles Gray's chambers on the Friday before the case began. I asked for the odds on the case, and was told 60/40 in favour of the damages going higher than £50,000. The feeling seemed to be that we could do much better and that we had a good case. I was under the impression that if we won and were only awarded £50,000, then I would lose the damages as they would just about cover the costs for which I would be liable. I was not advised to accept the payment in the court. So I decided to press on.

Finally, the first day of the trial arrived. In order to keep down the level of disruption to my colleagues in the Street I asked that they should be heard first. This was agreed.

Kelvin McKenzie didn't even bother turning up. Mr McKenzie is in my view a bully. He talks about the right to publish stories he describes as being in the public interest, but seems incapable of telling the difference between the public interest and what interests the public. He made no comment before, during or after my case. Ken Irwin had to do all the work in the witness box. And he was unable to verify a single statement that appeared in his article, I might add.

Anyway, we had a false start. The trial did not begin on the Monday, as expected, because another case over-ran, and we started on Tuesday.

Sara and myself stayed at the Waldorf Hotel in the Aldwych, which is within walking distance of the High Court. But we never did walk, because there was an incredible barrage of reporters waiting for us every morning. We had a suite at the Waldorf, consisting of two bedrooms and a sitting room, and the staff looked after us very well, which was a comfort.

Bernard Coral, who I've known ever since the early days of the Variety Club golf tournaments, gave us temporary membership of his club, the Wig and Pen, which is just opposite the High Court. It was very good of him. It meant we could go over there when we weren't needed in court, and as it was a private club the Press couldn't get in. But things didn't quite work out as intended. Because, instead of dashing out of the court and into the comparative privacy of a taxi, we had to get across the road through this most incredible mob of journalists and photographers. They pushed and shoved, they stopped the traffic, they battled with each other to get near us. Once, one photographer fell over and was simply trampled. This became a terrible ordeal.

That first day in court, they went through my colleagues, who were absolutely wonderful. Apart from fellow cast members, producer Mervyn Watson, Tom Elliott from the writers and Brian Mills, the director, also spoke for me.

There was one very funny moment early on when Amanda Barrie gave evidence. She spoke about how her character, Alma, had an affair with Ken Barlow. Chief Justice Waterhouse interrupted at this point with, 'Can I get this right, please? You're having an affair with – '

'No, no,' said Amanda, 'not *me*. My character.' Everyone burst out laughing. There was a lot of humour about that.

That afternoon I was called into the witness box. This was much quicker than I expected. Fortunately, Peter Carter-Ruck's team had briefed me beforehand. I had written a statement about how I felt when I read Irwin's article and what the libel meant to me personally and professionally. My brief was to be frank and clear, to remember to address the judge as 'My Lord' at all times, and to always say less rather than more. I was also told not to worry if I went wrong and to concentrate on the questions.

I felt nervous when I stepped into the box, but I was sure of the rightness of my case and in command of what I wanted to say. In fact, at one point, when Mr Eady, counsel for the defence, wanted to move on, I said, 'I'm sorry, no; I don't want to move on just yet. I haven't finished.' I felt quite comfortable saying that.

The court adjourned at 4.30. But I hadn't finished giving my evidence. Of course you've been sworn in and this means your legal team aren't allowed to talk to you. So we just went back to the hotel, had a meal in our room and watched a bit of television.

I had a pretty easy time of it in the witness box on Tuesday, and this may have lured me into a false sense of security, because Wednesday was much worse. I should point out that I was not complaining about the segment of Irwin's article that made reference to my life in the sixties. I didn't want to open that particular can of worms, which the tabloids would have loved. My concern was to clear my name of the slurs on my professionalism.

When I got into the box on Wednesday, Mr Eady held up a copy of the article with that passage marked out. 'You're not complaining about this section here,' he said. 'But I intend going through it, line by line, and question you about it.'

I was furious. I turned to the jury and said, 'That section of the article talks about things which supposedly happened twenty years ago. The sixties were a different time, and I admit I didn't behave well in those days. But that was before my present marriage. I don't wish to talk about that and as I'm not complaining about that I don't see why I should have to.'

Then I turned back to Eady and said, 'And you're no better than the paper you represent; you're no better than 'The Sun.' I was on the verge of tears by this time.

The judge sat back and allowed me to rant and rave, which in retrospect was a bit surprising. Just as surprising was the fact that Eady didn't pursue that line of cross-examination. But what he did do was ask that the court read that section of the article. That was an uncomfortable couple of minutes and he knew exactly what he was doing.

The following day, naturally, every tabloid carried *only* those allegations about my sexual activities in the sixties. Seeing myself splashed all over the front pages made me wish that I'd actually gone for it after all, and argued line for line with Eady. But of course that's what *The Sun* wanted me to do. It would have been a nice juicy diversion and served to blacken my name in the process. In fact the defence carried on plugging away about this sixties thing throughout the whole trial.

I came out of the witness box that day in a very emotional and distressed state. I just wanted the ground to swallow me up. I thought, Why am I here? How have I got to this? I was shaking, my pulse rate went up and stayed up for weeks afterwards. I went into a terrible state about the pressure of the whole case.

Alan McCarthy, an executive with Equity who came along as an observer, said, '*You* are on trial, Bill.' He was right. You're pulverised, pilloried and got at; it's what you have to go through. I knew this would happen, and I knew I was ready for it mentally and physically, but for some reason I wasn't ready for it emotionally. It hit me in a devastating way, and I'm still not 100 per cent certain why.

So that day in the witness box was absolutely awful. And

in the evening I had to get up to Granada to do two scenes. Everyone was wonderfully protective and supportive, but I was feeling very strange and bewildered. The whole world was talking about the case, it made headlines as far afield as New Zealand and Canada.

Indeed some of the coverage in the papers here was so near the knuckle that Charles Gray complained to the judge about it. Chief Justice Waterhouse remarked, 'Yes, I must say I was surprised to find it was dealt with in *The Times* today.' The only paper to come out of it honorably was the *Daily Telegraph*, which behaved impeccably; anyone who read the *Telegraph* would have known what my case was about, would have read a true picture of what went on. The *Guardian* and the *Independent* weren't too bad either, but the *Telegraph* was the best. But the others were absolutely horrible.

Because I wasn't there on the Thursday, Sara had to go into the box without me around to give her emotional support, and she ended up in tears. It was all just as upsetting for her.

One source of comfort was that we knew the children were being well cared for. Mrs Beavis, the headmistress of Verity's school, St Hilary's, personally took charge of her. William was looked after by a professional nanny called Sheila. We were extremely grateful to both of them for doing such a good job. William's school, the Ryleys, also sent a note of support.

As I said, we took a taxi to the court every morning. On that Thursday Sara had to go on her own, and the driver pulled up some way from the court entrance. He said he wouldn't go to the door because there was a crossing in front of it. Sara was frightened because the usual pack of reporters were hovering about. She almost pleaded with this driver to take her past saying that they were waiting for her, but he didn't believe her, until she got out! So she had to fight through the scrum alone.

But I must say that was the only taxi driver who was anything other than pleasant to us. All the others were great, and I think without exception they all wished us good luck as we went in. In fact we had so many expressions of good wishes from an amazing number of people, including the ushers, security guards and clerical staff in the court. People would shout to us from the other side of the street, wishing us well.

And, as with the death of Edwina, we were deluged with mail from well-wishers. I'm ashamed to admit that I was so shaken up following the trial that some of those letters never got answered. I would like to take this opportunity to thank everyone who wrote, and to apologise for not answering every one of them. They were so supportive, and really restored my faith in human nature.

I got back to London on the Friday and Ken Irwin went into the witness box. A point of contention was that he said I had once given him an official interview and I maintained I hadn't. This particular interview had nothing to do with the article I was suing over. But it was important to get the truth of it in order to establish Irwin's ethics and the methods he employed.

He swore that he had recorded an interview with me. After a great deal of prevarication he produced a transcript. Then, very reluctantly, a cassette tape. And, sure enough, there I was talking to Ken Irwin. I thought I'd gone mad. Because I genuinely had no recollection of doing the interview.

Then I remembered that the only time I'd spoken to him was at the grand opening of Stage One, Granada's new set built specially for the Street. There was a launch to which the Press were invited and I was representing the cast. After a question and answer session I went off to the buffet, got myself a plate of food, and wandered around the room chatting to people. At one point I found myself standing next to Ken Irwin. I was doing PR for the company on behalf of Stage One so of course I talked to anybody.

I had never particularly liked the guy, and never trusted him, but I had no specific reason not to talk to him, particularly on a day when I was speaking on behalf of the company and we were promoting our new studio. So I chatted to him as we were eating. And that was it.

He apparently had a tape-recorder concealed about his person. In court, he said it was an official interview. This was refuted entirely by our press officer, who said there would have had to have been permission for it and he would have arranged it. And in his view I would not have agreed anyway. He was right. Irwin said he had sat there holding the tape-recorder in his hand between him and me the whole time so I could see it. A total lie.

The fact that he'd recorded our chat without telling me was totally disgraceful. And of course there were no witnesses. People wouldn't remember, they were milling about and eating lunch. I had a plate of food myself. But if you have an interview with someone you go into your dressing room or somewhere equally private and quiet. On this tape you could hear the people in the background; someone actually came up and spoke to me in the middle of it. That isn't the way you conduct an interview.

To record me secretly like that was very underhand.

In court, *The Sun* and its publishing company apologised for the line in the article containing the words, '. . . hated by the cast.' Ken Irwin didn't. He kept going on that I was despised. He couldn't name the people who despised me, but yes, a lot of the cast did according to him.

My barrister said, 'How many?'

He said, 'A lot.'

'Roughly how many?'

'I'm not going to say.'

'Will you name any?'

'No, I won't.'

And so it went on, with absolutely no verification for anything he had put in the article.

The barristers summed up on the Friday afternoon and we thought the case would be over that day. But there wasn't time for the judge's summation and directions to the jury, so it was adjourned until the following Monday.

We had the whole weekend to stew and worry ourselves stupid. We stayed on in London, but I was in such a state of nervous tension I couldn't keep still. On the other hand we couldn't go out without being pestered by photographers. We felt like a pair of caged animals. I was permanently keyed-up and needed sedating or something, but did not take anything. Then of course the Sunday papers raked it up all over again.

During Justice Waterhouse's summary on the Monday morning I started to feel uneasy. It was a long summing-up, he went through the whole case, and when he got to the point of awarding damages he mentioned several times that there must be nothing punitive about them. My heart sank. Punitive damages was half the reason I was there. I could feel things slipping away.

Eventually the jury went out, and it was out for quite a long time; about an hour and three-quarters I think. By now the tension was getting unbearable. I just wanted to go away and not know anything about anything, and rest, and forget it.

The jury came back and the Clerk of the Court asked who it had found in favour of. The jury foreman said, 'The plaintiff,'

I had won. *The Sun*, Kelvin McKenzie and Ken Irwin had libelled me and now everyone knew it.

Then the foreman was asked for a damages figure.

'Fifty thousand pounds.'

It was beyond belief. The jury had awarded me the exact amount *The Sun* had paid into court. And the jury does not know how much has been paid into court. This was sheer coincidence. If it had said £50,000 and one *penny* I would have been in the clear.

I might have won the case, but I now had to pay the full costs of both sides, after the payment which was going to wipe out the £50,000. And to *The Sun* it was a financial pin-prick. Petty cash.

At the end of the day, having been through this *dreadful* experience, having been humiliated and having to pay for the privilege, it just didn't seem worth it. In so far as it's possible for a man to say this, I felt like I'd been raped. I had achieved a classic Pyrrhic victory. The newspapers can go on and on, libelling whoever they want, and there's not a thing anyone can do about it.

My counsel got up and started his plea for me to be awarded costs even though the damages matched the amount paid into court. In fact his argument was based on the damages being so meticulously balanced. The judge agreed and awarded me costs.

Why did I feel in such a state? Because it still wasn't right; I hadn't achieved what I set out to do in terms of teaching *The Sun* a lesson. And because my intuition told me that at the end of the day I wouldn't be getting those costs anyway.

This is what happens of course. You hear about these big libel cases and their massive awards. But they *always* go to appeal if it's over £50,000, and nearly always they are reduced. Something else you discover is that if you're awarded £50,000, you don't get £50,000. There is a kind of levy called court taxing. It takes the form of assessing the costs of a case and apportioning about a third of them to you.

Judges, and appeal judges particularly, seem to think awards in libel cases are ridiculously high. But given that it's the only system there is, and given that individuals who do have the courage to stand up and go through it are rare, I think it's darn right they should be high. They should be fifty times higher. The judges should listen to the people instead of criticising them.

Eighteen

The Sun appealed on the grounds that if the amount paid into court was matched by or was less than damages, it was normal practice for the plaintiff to pay costs. The appeal was heard in November, 1992, one year after the trial.

I had in the meantime developed an ulcer which required hospitalisation. Purely as a result of the pressures brought on by this business and I am still not fully recovered.

The panel of appeal consisted of Master of the Rolls Sir Thomas Bingham, and Justices Stuart Smith and Simon Brown. They all went on about vast damages paid to litigants. They said that if the amount paid into court is met by the damages, the costs must be paid by the plaintiff. They also said that at the end of the day the damages awarded were quite sufficient. To me it was an ice-cold judgment. Judges kept going on about ridiculously high amounts given by juries, but in my view it is the judges who are out of touch and the people are longing to tell them that it is time the excesses of the tabloids were stopped.

I was very unhappy with what they said. There wasn't a mention of the risks, the difficulties, the costs and the fears of individuals standing up to try to prove they have been libelled. I lost, on appeal, all costs. And I have to pay the costs of the appeal too. Where is the justice in that?

I was actually appalled by the attitude of the appeal judges going by the letter of the law rather than justice and oblivious to the behaviour of the tabloids. I've always respected the law as doing the best it can, and I think to some extent it does. But all I can say now is I want to keep away from it wherever possible.

What should be done about the libel laws? I'm not in agreement with censorship. There should be total freedom of speech and people should be able to read whatever they want. However, there is gross misbehaviour going on that is harming and damaging people, and the newspapers are making money out of it. I think a system of licensing newspapers, similar to the one applying to television and radio stations, could be the answer.

Every television company, for example, is subject to the ITC, an independent watchdog made up of good men and women not employed by the industry. The ITC, and its radio counterpart, oversee, among other things, conduct and behaviour. This is very different from censorship.

There should be a similar, *genuinely* independent body for the Press too, perhaps covering both newspapers and magazines. This body should be financed by the industry itself but stand quite apart from it. And it should have teeth. It would be able to impose really meaningful fines, and in extreme cases suspend a title's licence to publish for a day, a week or even permanently. I do not advocate the licences themselves being hard to obtain but, rather like a domestic television licence, it would be illegal to publish without one. And illegal to ignore the rulings of the commission that I propose.

I firmly believe that really substantial fines and the prospect of being unable to publish are the only things likely to bring the Press into line. But let me make it clear that I would not wish in any way to interfere with the Press's capacity to expose genuine wrong doing. Investigative journalism is a valuable part of our free society and should be, if anything, encouraged. I envisage the system I propose being applied only to intentional misinformation and the kind of mud-slinging all too prevalent in today's newspapers.

Maybe there could also be a kind of points system, based on the number of libel cases lost by a newspaper in any one year. Each case lost would equal a set period during which that paper could not publish.

I would like to see the equivalent of a small-claims court for libel cases. The amount of time and money even a modest case of libel or slander takes up at present is ridiculous. Such a court would not pay out vast sums in damages, or cost the earth for plaintiffs to use; in fact, initial advice could possibly be free. A court like this would have the added advantage of leaving the higher courts a little less cluttered and more able to concentrate on really serious criminal cases.

It would also eliminate the anomaly of legal aid being unavailable to fight libel cases, which ensures that such actions are restricted to people able to afford them. This is an injustice given that people from all walks of life are regularly dragged through the gutter by the Press. I understand why legal aid is not granted for libel cases – there would no doubt be frivolous actions, and even genuine ones would probably deplete the funds!

One other thing. There should be a *legal* obligation on newspapers to check with at least one independent source that what they print is true. I don't think that's asking too much. Obviously certain things would be difficult to verify, but the responsibility should be on the paper to check as best they can. Then, if they are taken to law on a point of fact, they have only to provide proof that they checked. This would actually be to their advantage, I think.

I suppose some people will say that I advocate these kind of measures out of spite or bitterness borne of my experience. This is honestly not the case. My brush with the Press and the legal system opened my eyes to a great injustice which I believe must be put right.

I also believe that bad behaviour, misinformation, bias and lies actually affect the functioning of our democracy. Because in order for a democracy to work properly the people have to be accurately and honestly informed. There is a danger of this being lost sight of. The behaviour of the less reputable elements of the print media is lowering people's judgement and their standard of thinking.

As to my relationship with the Press since the libel case, well, they just want to get on with business as usual. If anything, I have had more requests for interviews and offers to write articles than before the trial. Indeed, journalists even approached me during the case. I had notes slipped to me saying I would be paid tremendous amounts for my exclusive story. These offers were turned down. Had I been greedy, as was suggested by the defence during the trial and in a great deal of the Press coverage during and after it, I could have made a *lot* of money. *The Sun* had a disgraceful front page headline the next day – large enough to be announcing the start of World War Three – saying 'ROACHE DEMANDS £200,000'. This was untrue and apart from distorting and distracting from the case did me a lot of damage. All the major byline writers attacked me for being greedy the following day. When I lost the appeal the *Manchester Evening News* – up till then a paper I respected – had the massive headline 'GREEDY'. *The Sun* had achieved its aim of submerging the fact that I had won the case and been awarded £50,000 damages.

But I'm very, very wary now about my relationship with the Press, even if they say I can have power of approval on what gets published. Because I know this is usually only designed to lull you into a false sense of security. Inevitably what they print is incorrect or distorted and a journalist will respond with something like, 'Sorry, a sub-editor changed it on the night; I didn't know about it'. By which time it's too late to refute anything, of course.

I'm not saying I will never cooperate with the Press

again – publicity is part and parcel of being in the public gaze – but I would rather not be associated with it. If they improved their behaviour I would support them wholeheartedly.

I stood up for what I believe in. Irrespective of what happened in the sixties, I try to be an upright and moral person. *Of course* I fall short of that, and in the past I've fallen very short of it, but in this instance I was not just somebody out for a quick buck. I wouldn't have been so upset by the outcome if that had been my motivation. I just felt somebody had to stand up against these people. I had the opportunity to do so and it would have been cowardly if I hadn't taken it.

There's a little saying which I think sums up the state of the Press in this country quite nicely. It goes something like this – members of the government read *The Times*. People who think they should be in the government read the *Telegraph*. People who think they know what the government should be doing read the *Guardian*. People who think the government should be somebody else read the *Express*. People with no particular interest in who's in the government at the moment read *Today*. And people who read *The Sun* don't care who runs the government so long as she's got big tits.

It is a sad fact of life today that lawyers are rarely concerned with justice, doctors are not healers, and vicars are rarely spiritual men.

Nineteen

The demands of family life and animals leave little time for socialising but we do enjoy a meal out. We regularly meet Fred and Elsie Dover at the Holiday Inn, Manchester. Fred is the president for the Littleborough and Saddleworth Conservative Association and we frequently meet the MP Geoffrey Dickens there, who is wonderfully entertaining. Fred and Elsie are very good friends.

Other than family and old family friends we are probably closest to Betty and her sister and Freda Driver. Apart from being godparents and meeting socially never a day goes by but there is a knock on my dressing room door and a cheerful, 'Its me!' heralds Betty coming in for a chat. They are two wonderful people.

The Granada Studios Tour was created by David Plowright and John Williams and is hugely successful being the only thing of its kind in this country. It is a wonderful family day out showing how television programmes are made, and special effects produced; there are shows and entertainments, shops, restaurants, the giant room, a jungle, the House of Commons, a walk down Baker street, Downing Street and of course Coronation Street. William and Verity love it. 'How do you manage to film when tours are walking down Coronation Street,' I am frequently asked. The Tour does not operate on a Monday and that is when we shoot our exterior shots. These are shot out of sequence of course and the rest of the episodes are recorded in the studio on Thursday and Friday, continuity being the major concern. Wardrobe checks the continuity of clothes, position of coat collar and tie etc., polaroid cameras are the main aid for this. Make-up does the same, with hair being the major problem particularly on windy days. If it is raining, then before recording the studio scenes we have water sprayed on us. Many years ago having filmed walking up the Street and entering my house on the Monday I absent mindedly had a haircut on the Wednesday and then recorded coming through the door into my house on the Thursday. This must go down as the quickest haircut on record. There was nothing the continuity girls could do about that, but as my hair is always a bit casual, shall we say, by running my fingers through it as I entered we got away with it. I won't mention any names but I would like to say that all the wardrobe and make-up teams are very professional, hard working and delightful. You would not think that arriving at 7 a.m. on a Sunday morning for a make-up call was the best start to the day, but I always leave the department not only looking better but feeling better from their warmth and friendliness.

There have been various changes in *Coronation Street* over the years, but the biggest was when we went from two to three episodes a week.

This was a brave and difficult decision made by Steve Morrison and David Liddiment and created the most fundamental change to our working schedule since 'The *Street*' first began.

These changes altered the whole format of our work, and our schedule now includes Sundays, which is taken up with location filming. Prior to this the pace had been quite leisurely by comparison.

The very first day of Sunday location filming included six scenes between Ken and his new girlfriend Wendy Crozier (beautifully played by Roberta Kerr). A suitable house was found for this location belonging to a very pleasant middle aged couple and we called it 'The Wendy House'. One of the scenes was in the bedroom, with Ken finishing getting dressed and Wendy doing her make-up and Ken talking about having to go and see Deidre to get some of his belongings. Between scenes we often have to do a wardrobe change and I went into the room allocated to me to change my clothes. I was just about to start when Pam from wardrobe came in and said, 'Bill, the Director said knickers only for this scene please'.

I was not worried about the morality of this but being overweight – a continual problem since giving up smoking twenty years ago – I did not want to look like a stranded whale lying there. My old friend Brian Mills assured me it would look good and said I could look at the playback afterwards. He was right, as always, and it did add a new dimension to the scene. I spent a lot of my time apologising to the owners of the house about using it for immoral purposes, but they seemed to be thoroughly enjoying it.

Another question we are often asked is 'Do you watch it?'. The answer to this is yes. Even though we know what happens we can enjoy it and of course we have never seen the finished product as a lot is shot out of sequence. One example of this was a scene between Ken and Tracey leading up to Ken attempting suicide on New Year's Eve. It started with Ken and Tracey having a row in Ken's flat (shot on Thursday), followed by Ken running after her down his stairs (shot independently in a separate unit on Friday), then chasing her down the street (shot on Monday), and finally having a tearful session at the bottom of Deidre's stairs (shot late on Friday). So I had not the remotest idea what this would look like when it was all put together as one scene.

When we went to three episodes there was some concern about whether we could maintain the same standard. It used to be that we would run a strong story – Ken Barlow and Len Fairclough having a punch-up in the pub, say – then that finished and the following week you were on to something else. And sometimes in that new story you'd find Ken and Len standing next to each other in the Rovers' chatting as if nothing had happened. Nevertheless you were on to another story and it would run for three or four weeks before moving on to the next.

The main change in story structure when we went to three episodes was that instead of telling one major story in the classic, linear sense – literally as a serial – we suddenly had a number of strong threads running parallel. No longer did we have a central plot with incidentals going on around it.

We now had the opportunity to have good, meaty stories occurring all along the Street, involving the Duckworths, Ken and Deirdre, Mike and Alma, Gail and Martin or whoever. And these stories had no time limit to them, so we weren't dependent on one finishing so another could begin.

Far from the quality dropping and the Street drying up, this enriched it; we actually seemed to get a kick, a rush of adrenalin to the system when we went to three episodes. The new lease of life was quite extraordinary. We thought maybe it would settle and tiredness creep in after a while. On the contrary, the momentum and creativity just keep flowing. Moving to three episodes was more than a change, it was a quantum leap, and possibly the best thing to happen to *Coronation Street* since colour.

Welcome it or not, you have to accept change. There's no point in saying you don't like it and burying your head in the sand. The future is coming at us faster and faster. In television, as in everything else, we have to move forward, and hopefully try to keep standards and quality in step with the new technology.

Choice is going to be the buzz word of the future. Because cable is going to come along and hit us right between the eyes. It will totally revolutionise our way of life. Up to now, television viewers have been virtually a captive audience, with just a choice of four channels, although video and satellite have expanded this somewhat. But soon we are all going to have multiple choices, with thirty, forty or fifty channels available, and people will *have* to become more selective. One result of this fragmentation of audiences will probably be that high viewing figures for particular programmes will not automatically be there for the picking.

If we're going to have so many channels and so many choices, what will be on offer? Is everyone going to go for the cheapest product? Will the lowest common denominator rule? This is my fear. But we have to go along with change. You can't deny it or avoid it. The new communications technology is rather like the nuclear bomb – it's *there*. What all of us in the industry have to do is make sure morality and quality stands alongside innovation.

Coronation Street is not immune to any of these incredible developments. Our new management has a very, very difficult job in the face of the turbulent waves that are going to be coming at it. Things will not be easy for the management or us. But I am confident that Granada, *Coronation Street* and all of us will survive well into the twenty-first century.

The Street has always been rich in characters and this is as true today as it always was. But from time to time looking back over the thirty-three years to Ena, Annie and Elsie it only seems like yesterday and yet it is hard to believe that I was that young slim man. Sometimes I half expect them to walk through the door, to hear Uncle Albert grumble and Hilda to shriek 'Stanley'. They are very persistent ghosts.

Index